M
TRADING
AND OVERSOLD
CONDITIONS

This 3-hours reading will make you a successful trader in Equity and Forex markets

P. Arul Pandi

PROWESS
PUBLISHING

Copyright © 2022, P. Arul Pandi
All rights reserved.

No part of this publication may be reproduced or transmitted in any form or by any means, electronic or mechanical, including photocopy, recording or any information storage and retrieval system now known or to be invented, without permission in writing from the publisher, except by a reviewer who wishes to quote brief passages in connection with a review written for inclusion in a magazine, newspaper or broadcast.

Published in India by Prowess Publishing,
YRK Towers, Thadikara Swamy Koil St, Alandur,
Chennai, Tamil Nadu 600016

ISBN: 979-8-4171-3086-1

Library of Congress Cataloging in Publication

Contents

About the Author v
Disclaimer vi
Introduction. vii

PART I 1
1. Moving Averages 3
2. Average Directional Index (ADX). 10
3. Support and Resistance. 15
4. Pivot Points. 21
5. Fibonacci Retracements and Extensions 24
6. Divergences 31

PART II 35
1. Relative Strength Index. 37
2. Moving Average Convergence and Divergence (MACD). 48
3. Bollinger Bands 61
4. Stochastic Indicator. 72
5. Williams %R. 85
6. Accumulation Distribution 91
7. On-Balance Volume 99

8.	Money Flow Index..............................	105
9.	Commodity Channel Index......................	112
10.	Chande Momentum Oscillator..................	120

Conclusion... 124

About the Author

Mr. P. Arul Pandi is a retired executive of a bank owned by the Government of India. He has been into stock trading for more than three decades. He has been regularly conducting hands-on training programs on stock trading for ambitious traders. His success in trading with various technical tools and techniques and his penchant for teaching trading strategies resulted in his earlier books titled "Day Trading Techniques without Technicalities" and "Don't Trade before Learning These 14 Candlestick Patterns". These books have been receiving encomiums from traders and scholars in the trading field.

Author's contact details:
Mail: arulpandi58@gmail.com

Disclaimer

This book is for educational purpose only and should not be construed as an offer of advisory services. Nothing in this book should be construed as trade/investment advice or recommendation of any kind. You should not rely on any statement made in this book for trading on any instrument like stocks, futures and commodities. You are solely responsible for your decision to invest or trade in the stock market or buy or sell any specific share. Information presented in this book should not be regarded as a complete analysis of the subject discussed. If you need advice on investment or trading upon which you intend to rely in the course of your financial, business or legal affairs, you are advised to consult a competent financial advisor/consultant. All trading and investment strategies have the potential for profit as well as loss. You are solely responsible for any of your decision to buy or sell or invest in any stock, futures, commodities or currencies or any such instrument. All expressions of opinion reflect the judgment of the author as on the date of publication and are subject to change. The publisher and the author accept no liability for any loss or damage of any kind that may result from your trading and investment in stocks, futures, commodities and forex markets.

Introduction

What are Overbought and Oversold assets?

An overbought stock is one that has risen too much because of excessive buying and is probably *ripe for a fall*. An oversold asset is one that has fallen too much because of excessive selling and is probably *ripe for a rise*.

What takes an asset to overbought and oversold conditions?

Traders often tend to overreact to news, earnings releases, rumours and other market-moving events and make abnormally heavy buying or selling, and this carries prices too far in a particular direction.

Implication of overbought and oversold conditions:

When the demand for the stock exceeds its supply, price moves up. The up move continues, the price rises too much and reaches the level beyond which the buyers are not prepared to buy but choose to book profit. A price pullback is likely. Likewise, when the supply of the stock exceeds the demand for it, the price falls. The downtrend continues and the price falls too much and reaches the level beyond which the sellers are not prepared to sell but choose to book profit. A price bounce is likely.

However, even when the stocks have gone up too much, it does not mean that they have reached the peak and won't continue going up anymore. A stock may appear to be overbought because of up move during a long stretch of consecutive days but it may still continue the up move and become more overbought. Similarly, a stock may appear to be oversold because of continuous fall during a long stretch of consecutive days but the stock may continue to fall many more days and become more oversold. We, therefore, have to identify the peaks of markets to go short and the bottoms of markets to go long to take advantage of reversals that occur after overbought/oversold conditions.

There are two different ways of analysing financial assets, assessing their worth and predicting their future direction of price. They are fundamental analysis and technical analysis.

Fundamental Analysis vs. Technical Analysis

The objective of fundamental analysis is to arrive at the 'fair value' of a stock. For this purpose, financial analysts study financial and economic factors that have a bearing on the company's business. They study the Government's attitude towards the industry by way of import-export policy, taxation policy, subsidy policy, etc. They analyse the company's financial statements such as balance sheets, profit & loss accounts statements and cash and funds flow statements. They also look into the company's projections of turnover and profit and orders on hand. Thus the analysts study all the aspects that have a bearing on the company's profit, arrive at the "fair" value of the company's stock and determine whether the stock is fairly valued, over-valued or under-valued and take positions accordingly.

But technical analysts are of strong opinion that such analyses are unnecessary exercise; they strongly believe that historical price trends repeat themselves and hence previous levels of open, high, low, close and volume can be used to determine where the price is heading to and whether the stock is overbought or oversold.

What does this book do for you?

Though technical analysis is considered the best way of identifying overbought and oversold conditions, most of the traders are scared of seeing stock charts with candlesticks of different shapes and colours and line curves in different colours rising, falling and crossing one another. Here comes this book as a guide. This book discusses a few of the most reliable technical tools and indicators that help to identify and respond to trade signals at the right time in overbought and oversold conditions and earn optimal profit.

The technical indicators chosen for this purpose have been carefully drawn from all the five categories of indicators (which are detailed below) so that the buy-sell signals generated by these indicators are validated and are reliable and trades based on them are consistently profitable.

Categories of Technical Indicators

The following are the five categories of technical indicators:

1) **Trend Indicators:** These indicators tell us whether a trend actually exists, and if it exists, which direction it is heading to. This helps traders trade securities that are trending (up or down). We will discuss in this book the following trend indicators:

    Moving Averages
    Average Directional Index

2) **Momentum Indicators (Oscillators):** Oscillators indicate the extent of momentum that is building up on a particular stock. When price rises, oscillators move higher. When price falls, oscillators move lower. This indicates to us how strong the trend is and whether a reversal is imminent as it is highly probable that when oscillators reach extreme levels, prices will tend to move back to the mean. We will cover in this book the following momentum indicators:

    Relative Strength Index
    Stochastic Indicator
    Moving Average Convergence and Divergence
    Williams %R
    Chande Momentum Oscillator

3) **Volatility Indicators:** These indicators tell us how large the upswings and downswings are for the asset under

consideration. Traders can earn by trading only if the price is volatile, that is, if the price goes up and down. The following Volatility Indicator is discussed in this book:

    Bollinger Bands

4) **Volume Indicators:** Volume precedes price. There are a number of indicators which tell us whether volume is flowing into or out of a stock. Eventually they work well in predicting future movement of the stock. The following Volume Indicators are discussed in this book:

    On-Balance Volume
    Money Flow Index
    Accumulation Distribution
    Commodities Channel Index

5) **Support/Resistance Indicators:** We will cover in this book the following technical tools which clearly show to us support and resistance zones:

    Pivot Points
    Fibonacci Retracements and Extensions

Now let us go to individual chapters and learn the technical indicators and win trades.

PART I

This part of the book explains in separate chapters a few technical tools and concepts which are helpful to traders while deploying certain major technical indicators in trading overbought and oversold conditions. A person who wants to get into securities trading must know what is what of these tools.

1. Moving Averages

Moving Average (MA) is a technical analysis tool that constantly averages a security's prices over a period of time and thereby smooths out price data. This smoothing effect of the moving average gives a clear indication of the direction of the price of the security – up or down or sideways- over a specific period of time. If the moving average curve is rising, it means price is rising; if the moving average curve is falling, it means price is falling. If the curve is directionless and moving sideways, it indicates that the market is in a range.

Moving Average Length

Commonly used moving average lengths (also called "look back periods" and "timeframes") are 10, 20, 50, 100 and 200.

When an asset begins an uptrend, short term moving averages will start rising much earlier than the long term moving averages. That is, an MA with a short timeframe will react much quicker to price changes than a long term MA.

CHART

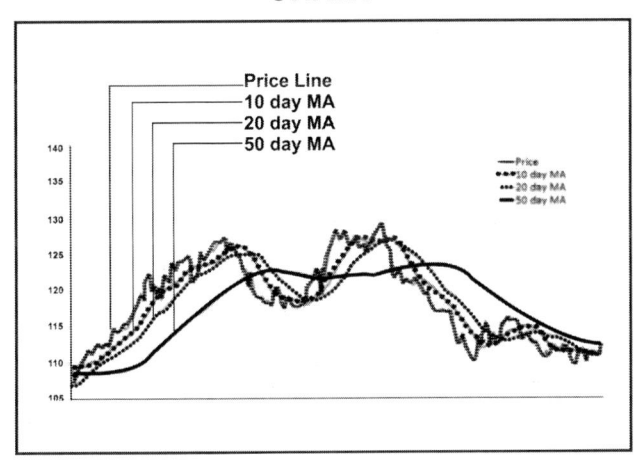

In the above chart, there are three moving average lines- the 10-day moving average line, the 20-day moving average and the 50-day moving average. It can be observed that (i) the 10-day moving average is the closest line to the price curve, (ii) it tracks the actual price more closely than the longer period moving averages, (iii) it has the maximum number of peaks and troughs, (iv) it generates many more "reversal" signals than a 30-day moving average and (v) the 30-day moving average is the farthest away from the price curve and the smoothest of the three lines.

From the above, one can infer that short period MA like 10-day MA will be suitable for day trading and longer-term MA is suitable for long-term traders.

Types of Moving Averages

There are different types of moving averages. The most commonly used types of moving averages are Simple Moving Averages and Exponential Moving Averages.

Simple Moving Average

A 10-day Simple Moving Average (SMA) adds up the 10 most recent daily closing prices and divides it by 10 to create a new value of average each day.

Exponential Moving Average (EMA)

Exponential Moving Average (EMA), also called exponentially weighted moving average, is a type of moving average (MA) that assigns more weightage to recent data points. That is, each term in the EMA's period has an exponentially greater weightage than its previous term. There are also a few variants of EMA which use variables like open, high, low or median price instead of using the closing price.

Simple Moving Average vs Exponential Moving Average

If you plot a 50-day SMA and a 50-day EMA on the same chart, you'll notice that the EMA reacts to price changes faster than the SMA does as more weightage is given to more recent price data in calculating EMA and hence the EMA is more dependable. As EMA depicts the recent performance of the security more clearly and accurately, it makes a better moving average trading strategy.

The following chart shows how SMA and EMA of the same look-back period respond to price.

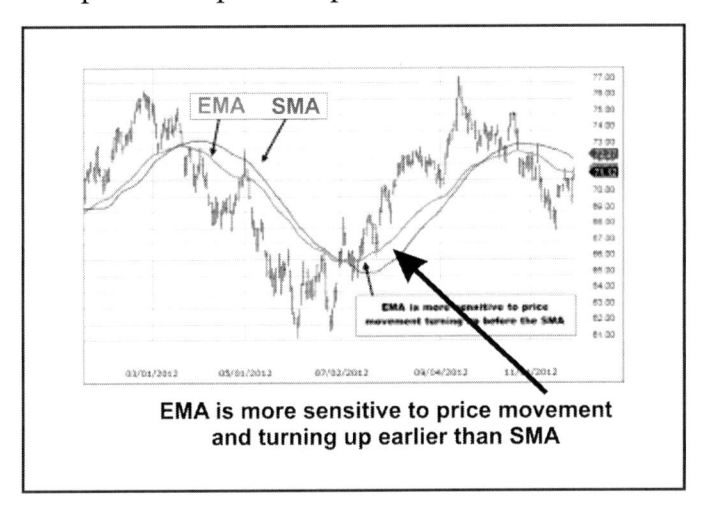

EMA is more sensitive to price movement and turning up earlier than SMA

Interpretation of position and movement of Moving Averages:

1) If the price is consistently above or below a moving average line, you can rest assured that the price trend is strong and the trade can be allowed to run as it is.
2) Direction of MA line reflects the market trend. Generally, if the MA on a daily chart is on strong uptrend, day traders will think of going long only. If the MA line on the daily chart is on downtrend, traders will consider going short only.
3) The farther the price can pull away from a moving average, the stronger the current trend is. That is, when price curve is at higher level than the Moving Average curve and the price curve is rising, the price trend is said to be bullish.
4) When the price line crosses the moving average line, it signals a potential trend reversal depending upon the direction of the MA.

5) The longer the price stays on one side of the moving average without touching the moving average, the stronger the trend.
6) The slope of a moving average is important. When the price is above the MA and the MA is angled up, it signals a strong trend with prices rising faster than the historical averages. If the MA is angled down, the price is moving down. If the MA is moving sideways, the price is likely to be fluctuating in a range.
7) A moving average acts as a good support in downtrend and a good resistance in uptrend. Of course, the price may not respect the moving average always in this way, and it may cross the moving average considerably if the trend is so strong.
8) Another important thing to note in MA chart is the rate of change happening between bars. If the price line in a strong uptrend starts losing momentum and starts falling, the MA's rate of change from bar to bar will be declining, and this declining rate of change of the MA itself is a good indicator of reversal of trend.

Trading Strategies—Crossovers

Crossovers of moving averages of different timeframes provide traders with good trade opportunities as narrated below.

1) Price and MA crossover

When the price crosses a moving average, it is a signal of trend reversal.

- Buy when the price curve cuts the short term moving average curve from below.
- Sell when the price curve cuts the long-term moving average curve from above.

2) Short period and long period MAs crossover

Crossovers of short MAs and long MAs provide profitable trading strategies. The following are a few combinations of different types of moving averages with different look-back periods:

a) Short period SMA and long period SMA crossover

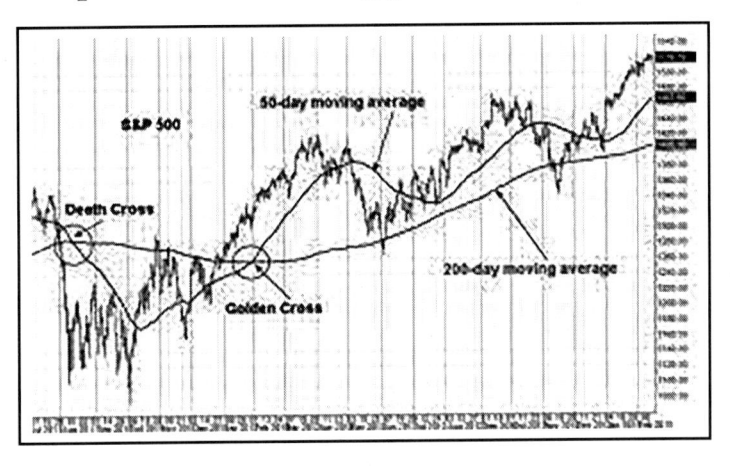

When the shorter-term MA crosses the longer-term MA from below, it indicates that the trend is upward, and it is a buy signal. Crossover of SMA (50) and SMA (200) is highly valued by traders. When the SMA (50) crosses the SMA (200) from below, it is called a 'Golden Cross', and when the SMA (50) crosses the SMA (200) from above, it is called a 'death cross'.

b) Short period EMA and long period EMA crossover

Similarly, when the short period EMA crosses the longer period EMA from above, it is a bearish signal. Most of the day traders use 12-day and 26-day EMAs which are also used to create MACD.

c) Short-period EMA and longer period SMA crossover

Another good moving average crossover is short period EMA vs. long period SMA. When short period EMA crosses long period SMA from below, it is a buy signal, and when the short period EMA crosses long period SMA from above, it is a sell signal.

3) Triple Moving Averages Crossover Strategy

Entering a trade too early may involve the risk of trading on false signal leading to losing trade, whereas entering a trade after much caution and time lag may make us miss a sizable portion of profit. Triple Moving Averages Crossover Strategy addresses this issue by giving mostly right trade signals at the right time.

This strategy deploys three moving average lines of different timeframes- small-period, medium-period and long-period moving average lines. Buy signal is generated early as soon as a new trend emerges when the small-period MA line crosses the medium-period from below provided the price is above the long-term MA. Sell signal is generated when the opposite events occur, that is, the short-term MA line crosses the medium-term MA from above and the price is below the long-period MA.

Our main concern is whether the price line is above or below the long-term MA. Never go long when the price is below the long-term MA line. Similarly, never go short when the price is above the long-term MA.

The combination of 5-, 8-, and 13-days simple moving averages (SMAs) also proves to be a good day trading crossover strategy as this is a Fibonacci-tuned setting.

4) Strategy of taking positions in a staggered manner

In this strategy, the trader will go long for a certain amount when the short-period MA crosses medium-period MA from below and will be taking long positions for a certain more amount when the short-period MA crosses the long-period MA from below, and again will be taking some long positions when the medium-period MA also crosses the long-period MA from below. The trader will exit his positions if any trend reversal is noticed.

5) Moving Average Ribbon

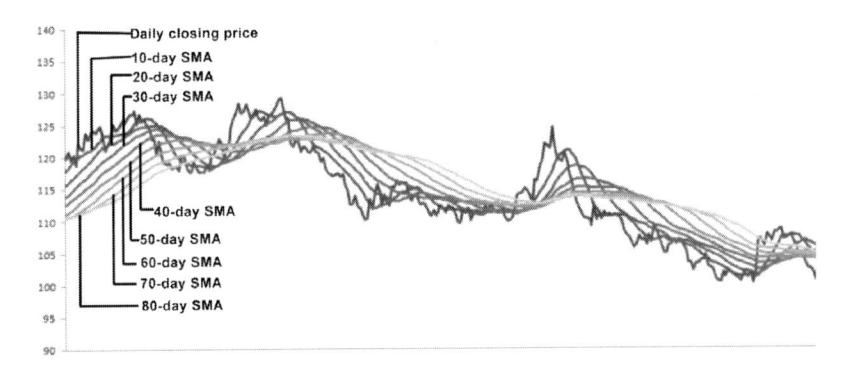

Those traders who do not want to follow numerous charts with different logic, settings and parameters prefer this strategy. They place a large number of SMAs, say, 6 SMAs on the chart. Each SMA's timeframe will be a multiple of one another so that the chart will give a comparable picture of the market trend.

As you may agree, all the SMA lines will travel in the same direction if the trend is strong.

Now traders are to determine how many crossovers among the MAs will be buy-sell signals. They buy when short-term MAs cross long-term MAs from below. Likewise, they go short when short-term MAs cross long-term MAs from above.

Limitations of trading with Moving Averages

1) When the price is highly volatile, too many trade signals will be generated. When that is the case, it is better to avoid trading at all.
2) Similarly, if two or more MAs are moving almost parallel to each other touching now and then causing weak crossovers without indication of a clear trend, trading on the signals may be avoided.
3) As moving averages are formed by historical data, they are lagging indicators i.e., their movements lag behind the movements of price and volume in charts and they do not predict price trend. (Lag is the time taken by a moving average to signal an impending trend reversal.)

2. Average Directional Index (ADX)

Why Average Directional Index?

"Trend is your friend" is the cardinal principle of stock trading. Yes, most of the market strategists recommend that a stock trader should buy only if market is rising and should go short only when the market is falling. But how to find out whether the currently prevailing price trend of a stock is strong enough to buy or short? Here the technical tool Average Directional Index (ADX) comes in handy. ADX enables us to avoid fakeouts. ADX is much helpful to the traders who want to trade only strong trends and to exit the trade if and when the trend weakens to avoid getting caught by a change in trend.

What does ADX do?

ADX shows to us whether the market is trending or range-bound and, if trending, how strong the trend is. Thus the indicator helps us filter out non-trend trades and avoid unproductive trades and frequent whipsaws. Unlike RSI, Moving Averages and Bollinger Bands, the ADX Indicator doesn't tell us whether the price is trending up or down but it measures the **strength** of the current trend- whether uptrend or downtrend. That is, ADX is non-directional and it does not tell you in which direction the price is moving.

The ADX indicator quantifies the strength of a trend in a range of zero to 100 by rising in uptrends as well as downtrends. (ADX cannot, therefore, have a negative value). The closer the ADX gets to 100, the stronger the trend is.

In the following chart, you can observe that as the "strength" of the "declining price trend" is increasing, the ADX line is also rising.

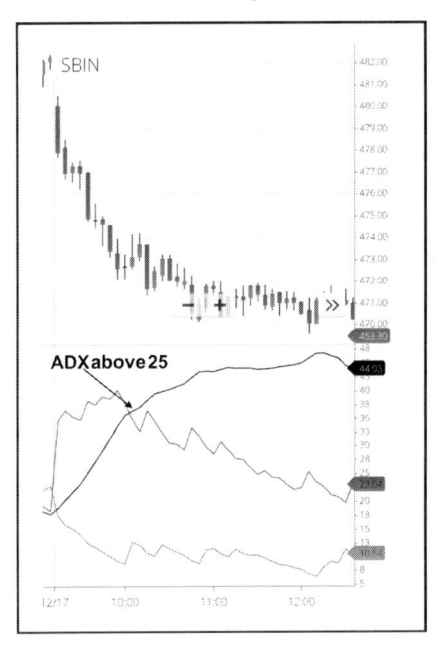

In the following chart, you can observe that price trend is sharply upward and the ADX line is also sharply upward.

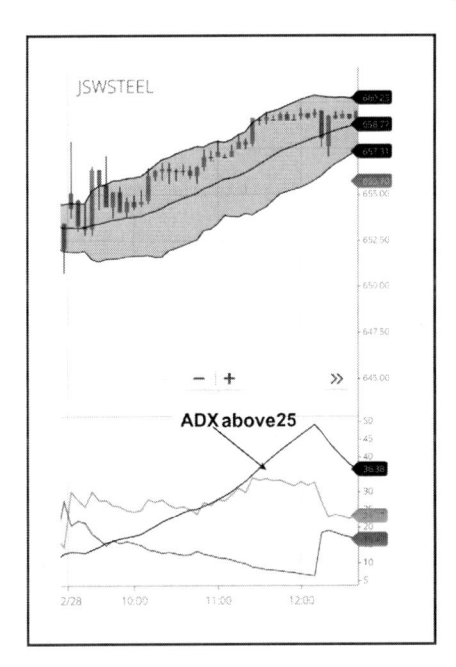

The following chart shows that when the price is moving sideways/range-bound, the ADX value is less than 25.

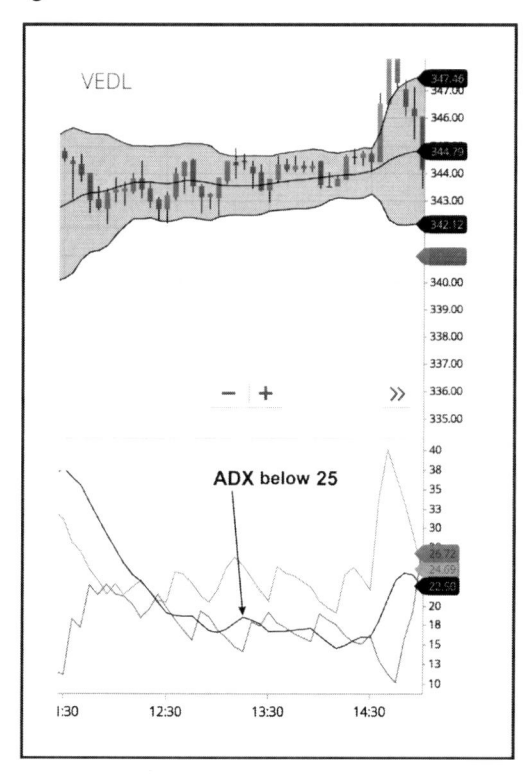

What do the Positive and Negative Directional Indicators do?

Though trading softwares make the ADX indicator readily available so that you need not manually calculate it, it is better to understand how the indicator is calculated.

ADX makes up a technical trading system (ADX / DMI) along with four other indicators. To calculate the ADX, the + and − directional movements, or DM, are determined by calculating the "up-move," or current high minus the previous high, and the "down-move," or current low minus the previous low. If the up-move is greater than the down-move and is greater than zero, the +DM equals the up-move; otherwise, it equals zero. If the down-move is greater than the up-move and greater than zero, the −DM equals the down-move;

otherwise, it equals zero. The Positive Directional Indicator, or +DI, equals 100 times the exponential moving average of +DM divided by the average true range over a given number of time periods. Traders usually use 14 periods. The Negative Directional Indicator, or −DI, equals 100 times the exponential moving average of −DM divided by the average true range (ATR). The ADX indicator itself equals 100 times the exponential moving average of the absolute value of (+DI minus −DI) divided by (+DI plus −DI).

When all is said and done, I advise traders to ignore the +DI line (which is green in colour) and the −DI line (which is red in colour) as trading based on these indicators will most probably lead to loss only. Let us study and deploy only the ADX line (which is in black colour) for taking trade decisions.

Interpretation of ADX values and ADX line's direction:

- If both the price and the ADX indicator are going UP, it is a case of a bullish trend.
- If the price is going down and the ADX indicator is going UP, then it is a case of a bearish trend.
- A falling ADX does not mean that a trend is ending.
- A rising ADX indicates that the prevailing trend is gaining strength.
- New highs on the ADX signal a healthy trend.
- Lower highs on the ADX signal losing strength.
- An ADX that is flat or heading down signals a range market.
- If ADX is between 0 and 25, the trend is weak or absent i.e., non-trending, and the stock is moving sideways. To be avoided for trend trading.
- If ADX goes above 25, trend is strong and trend trading can be taken up.
- If ADX peaks are above 25 but the ADX peaks are getting lower and lower, it means that the trend is losing momentum though the uptrend remains intact.

- If ADX is between 25 and 50, it indicates a strong trend and big moves (up or down as the case may be) tend to happen.
- If ADX is between 50 and 75, the trend is very strong. It is a rare occasion and it indicates exhaustion.
- If ADX is between 75 and 100, it is an extremely strong trend; it is very rare. Such trends are not sustainable and traders should, therefore, anticipate trend reversal.

Trading with ADX

1) Trend trading

First, use ADX to determine whether prices are trending or non-trending. Then choose the appropriate trading strategy for the condition.

In trending conditions, entries are made on pullbacks and taken in the direction of the trend.

- If both the price and the ADX indicator are going up and ADX value is above 25, it is a buy signal.
- If the price is going down and the ADX indicator is going UP and the ADX value is above 25, it is a sell signal.

2) Divergence

If price makes a higher high while ADX makes a lower high, it is a case of negative divergence, i.e., non-confirmation that warns that trend momentum is changing and that may lead to a trend reversal and stop loss should be in place or partial profit should be booked. The phenomenon of divergence has been explained in detail in a separate chapter.

3) Confirming reliability of breakouts

Breakout in range happens when a major change happens in the balance between the supply and demand for the stock. If the ADX value is above 25 and if the ADX crosses to a higher level, we can believe that the breakout is not a fake one and that the price will continue in the direction of the breakout.

3. Support and Resistance

As you know, price of an asset is determined by the interaction of demand and supply forces. Price falls till the point where demand outstrips supply. This is the point of support from which price will start rising. As the price declines towards support and gets cheaper, buyers become more inclined to buy and sellers become less inclined to sell. By the time the price reaches the support level, it is believed that demand will overcome supply and prevent the price from falling further. In other words, support is the price level at which demand is considered to be strong enough to prevent the price from declining further.

The price rises till supply outstrips demand. When the supply outstrips demand, prices will start falling; it is the point of resistance.

To be brief, Support and resistance levels are the levels that prices find it difficult to break through and once the support is broken properly, the support level will act as a resistance level for that particular stock and vice versa.

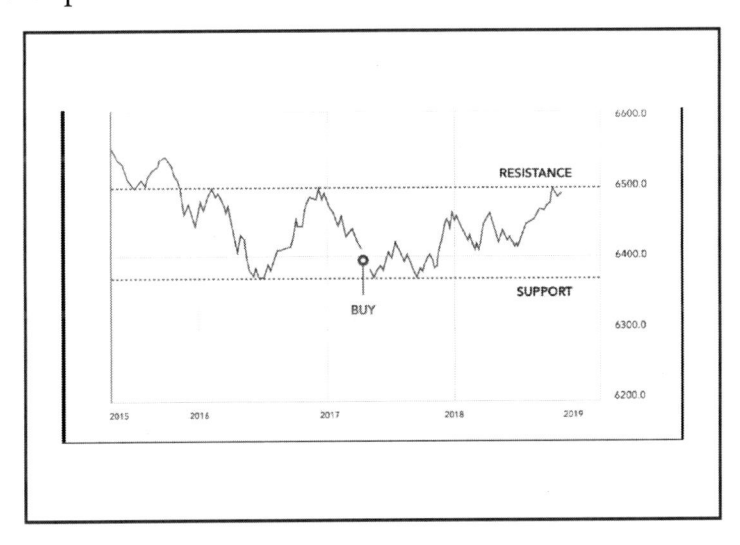

By this time, you would have understood that the basic trading strategy with the support and resistance concepts is to buy a security when price is at the support zone and to sell when price is at the resistance zone.

Please note that support and resistance levels do not refer to exact amount of price but are only territories/zones.

Types of Support and Resistance

i) Fixed Support and Resistance Levels
    These support and resistance levels are fixed levels and they do not keep changing with time and price trend often. Round numbers like Rs. 1000 or $100 and previously touched important price points such as 52-Week High are examples of fixed support and resistance levels.

ii) Dynamic Support and Resistance Levels
    Some technical indicators like moving averages and Bollinger Bands exhibit support and resistance levels that change with price and time. These levels are called Dynamic Support and Resistance Levels.

iii) Semi-Dynamic Support and Resistance Levels
    Technical tools like Pivot Points, Fibonacci lines and trend lines indicate support and resistance points that often change to pre-determined levels in tune with changes in time and price. These are called Semi-Dynamic Support and Resistance Levels.

Ways to determine Support and Resistance Levels

Support and resistance levels in the markets can be identified in the following ways:

1) Pivot Points

Pivot points system is a technical analysis indicator that uses a stock's past values of opening, high, low and close to forecast support and resistance levels. The previous day's trading range values are the inputs for obtaining today's pivot points. Central pivot point (also called standard pivot point) is simply the average of the high, low and closing price of the previous day.

Central Pivot Point (P) = (High + Low + Close)/3

Many other pivot levels, that is, support and resistance levels are arrived at based on the Central Pivot Point as could be seen from the chapter on Pivot Points.

Most traders believe that the central pivot point is the main support and resistance level; they buy only when the price is above the pivot point and sell short only when the price is below the pivot point.

2) Fibonacci Levels

Fibonacci sequence is a never-ending series of numbers beginning from 0 and 1 arranged in such a manner that any particular number in the series is simply the summation of the previous two numbers as shown below:

0, 1, 1, 2, 3, 5, 8, 13, 21, 34, 55, 89, 144 and so on.

All the numbers after 5 in the above series cause certain ratios when they divide their succeeding numbers and also when they are divided by their preceding numbers. These ratios are called Fibonacci ratios, and these ratios prove to be effective support and resistance levels. (A detailed account of the Fibonacci concept and ways of using it in trading has been dealt with in a separate chapter under Part-I)

The Fibonacci ratios are used in trading in two different ways- Fibonacci retracements and Fibonacci extensions.

Fibonacci Retracement levels: Even when the present trend is likely to continue, the asset price usually retraces to one of the Fibonacci ratios viz., 61.8%, 38.2% and 23.6% and then resumes the previous trend. The levels 61.8%, 38.2% and 23.6% which lie within the range of 0 to 100 are called Fibonacci retracement levels. Fibonacci retracements help traders determine where a correction or pullback that is moving in the opposite direction of the main trend will come to an end. Thus the Fibonacci retracement levels help traders identify the best entry points at the earliest when a market is retracing. Fibonacci retracement lines will also act as support lines in uptrends, and resistance lines in downtrends.

Fibonacci Extension levels: The levels that are located after 100 (123.6%, 138.2%, 161.8%, etc) are called Fibonacci extension levels. For instance, if a security's price rises from Rs. 50 to 60 and then falls to Rs. 56, the downward move from Rs. 60 to Rs. 56 is a retracement, and if the price then resumes uptrend and rallies to 63, it is an extension. Fibonacci extensions indicate to traders the best possible price targets in a trendy market.

Fibonacci extension lines will also act as resistance lines in uptrends and support lines in downtrends.

The following chart shows how the price trend changes direction at support and resistance levels derived from the Fibonacci ratios.

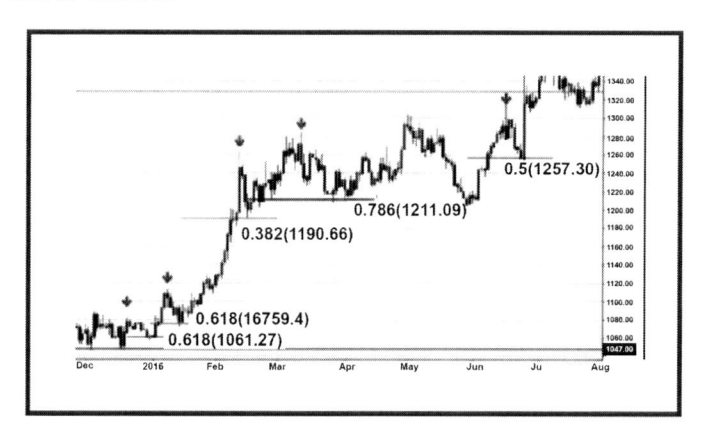

3) Peaks and Troughs

The most popular way of determining support and resistance levels is to simply note the apparent highs and lows on the chart. The lower lows and higher lows are considered support zones and the higher highs and lower highs are considered resistance zones.

4) Trendlines

Traders use trendlines to trade with the trend. When a security is in an uptrend, a trendline is drawn by connecting a low with subsequent higher lows and then extending the line to the future. This line will act as a support line. When a security is in a downtrend, a trendline is drawn by connecting one particular high with subsequent lower highs and then extending the line to the future. This line will act as a resistance line.

5) Frequently tested levels working as support and resistance levels

The more often the price touches a particular support or resistance level, the more important the level becomes. When prices keep touching a price level very often, more and more buyers will tend to treat that price level as support/resistance and base their trading decisions accordingly.

6) Prices in round numbers as support and resistance levels

Once a stock's price reaches a round amount like Rs. 100 and Rs. 1000, the stock price usually finds it a little difficult to move beyond that level as most traders are tempted to buy or sell stocks when the price is at a round number. Most stop-loss orders and trigger orders set by all sorts of traders including retail traders and mutual funds are placed at prices in round amounts rather than at prices such as Rs. 100.35. As huge number of orders are placed at the same level, these round numbers tend to act as strong price barriers. When a stock broker or a stock analyst gives his clients a recommendation to buy or sell a particular stock at a particular price which is normally in whole numbers like Rs. 110 and 125 and not like 101 and 103, a huge number of the clients will place orders at that round price, and consequently the price level will become good support and resistance level.

Trading with Support and Resistance levels

1) Breakout Trading

Support and resistance zones can often be breached. A support line breach means that that a downtrend has started and one can consider selling short; a resistance line breach means that an uptrend has started and one can consider going long. These breakouts often occur after a long period of consolidation and become the start of a new trend. Consequently, traders are able to enter trade at the early stage of the trend and reap maximum profits.

However, there is the danger of fake breakouts also; prices may cross the support/resistance zones but may immediately retrace to the pre-breakout level due to the fact that the momentum behind the breakout is weak. To avoid such loss-making trades, one should verify the strength of the trend with momentum indicators like MACD and ADX.

2) Range Trading

In range-bound markets i.e., non-trending markets, prices tend to oscillate between support zones and resistance zones. The frequently touched highs and lows during such range-bound movements will mostly act as resistance and support levels respectively. Traders can sell when the price reaches those resistance zones and buy when the prices reach support zones. It will be safer if the non-trending condition of market gets validated by an ADX reading of less than 25 and oscillators like Stochastic and RSI are in overbought/oversold conditions.

3) Trading on price rejection at support and recovery

Note down the support zones of strong stocks and resistance zones of weak stocks. (We are determined to avoid buying weak stocks and shorting strong stocks). Once such a zone of support or resistance is identified, the entry and exit points of a stock become clear to traders because when the price touches the support or resistance level, it either respects the support/resistance zone and retraces or continues the trend further to the next support/resistance level. When a strong stock is found falling towards a support area, be on the lookout for price rejection at the support area. Buy a when such price rejection occurs at the support level and after completion of a candle. When a weak stock is found rising, look for price rejection at resistance, and short it after the price rejection and after completion of a candle.

4. Pivot Points

Pivot points system is a technical analysis indicator that uses a stock's past values of opening, high, low and close to forecast support and resistance levels. That is, the previous day's trading range values are the inputs for obtaining today's pivot points.

Central pivot point (also called as base pivot point) is the average of the high, low and close of the previous day.

Central pivot point = (High + Low + Close)/3

The central pivot point is just one of the main support/resistance levels. If a stock's price is above the central pivot level, the stock is considered bullish. If the price is below the central pivot level, the stock is considered bearish.

How Pivot Points help in trading

Pivot points indicate support and resistance levels on the price chart. When price reaches a pivot level, the price level could meet a support/resistance or see a trend extension (breakout).

Different Kinds of Pivot Points

Here are five types of the most popular pivot points.

i) Standard Pivot points
ii) Fibonacci Pivot points
iii) Woodie's Pivot Points
iv) Camarilla Pivot Points
v) Denmark Pivot Points

We will discuss below two types of pivot points, namely, Standard Pivot Points and Fibonacci Pivot Points.

1. Standard Pivot Points

Central pivot point is the average of the high, low and closing price of the previous day.

$$\text{Central Pivot Point (P)} = (\text{High} + \text{Low} + \text{Close})/3$$

Other standard pivot points are calculated as shown below:

Support 1 (S1) = (P × 2) − High
Support 2 (S2) = P − (High − Low)
Support 3 (S3) = L − 2 × (H − P)
Resistance 1 (R1) = (P × 2) − Low
Resistance 2 (R2) = P + (High − Low)
Resistance 3 (R3) = H + 2 × (P − L)

2. Fibonacci Pivot Points

We already discussed in detail in an earlier chapter about Fibonacci retracement. Fibonacci retracement levels of 38.2% and 61.8% are mostly used as entry and exit points and also as support/resistance levels by traders in equity and forex markets.

Fibonacci pivot points based on the above Fibonacci levels are calculated as shown below:

Pivot Point (P) = (High + Low + Close)/3
Support 1 (S1) = P − {.382 × (High − Low)}
Support 2 (S2) = P − {.618 × (High − Low)}
Resistance 1 (R1) = P + {.382 × (High − Low)}
Resistance 2 (R2) = P + {.618 × (High − Low)}
Resistance 3 (R3) = P + {1 × (High − Low)}

Now let us see the trading strategies involving pivot levels:

1) If a stock is trading below the central pivot level i.e., (H+L+C)/3 even after 15 minutes since the opening of the market, you can consider shorting the stock. The rationale behind this is that if a stock could not move higher than the pivot value of the previous day even after the first 15 minutes of trading, there might be some sort of negative

sentiment against the stock in the market and selling pressure is probably more.

Stop loss can be fixed a little above the first resistance level so that a false breakout in price does not trigger the stop loss order causing avoidable loss.

Partial quantity may be covered by buying at the first support level and the remaining quantity may be covered by buying at the second support level.

For buy trade, follow the same rules but in reverse.

2) One need not bother much about the price reaching a pivot point. But if the price hesitates to move beyond the pivot point or if the price starts moving in the opposite direction, then you may consider trading in the new direction.

5. Fibonacci Retracements and Extensions

Fibonacci sequence is a never-ending series of numbers beginning from 0 and 1 arranged in such a manner that any particular number in the series is simply the summation of the previous two numbers as shown below:

0, 1, 1, 2, 3, 5, 8, 13, 21, 34, 55, 89, 144 and so on.

Presence of Fibonacci numbers in the nature

The Fibonacci numbers are nature's numbering system and Fibonacci sequence is a naturally occurring pattern; they appear everywhere in nature. We can also say that Fibonacci sequence is a naturally occurring pattern. This special sequence of numbers and the resultant ratios, called Fibonacci ratios, have features that are found in abundance in many natural phenomena.

The petals of many flowers are in Fibonacci numbers. Lilies have 3 petals, wild roses have 5 petals, and delphiniums have 8 petals. Seeds in many plants are in Fibonacci number as nature tries to provide an optimum number of seeds on flower heads filling space efficiently with no congestion at the center and no gap anywhere on the flower head. In Sunflowers, seeds are arranged in spirals, and the spirals are in both clockwise and anticlockwise directions. The number of the clockwise spirals and of the anticlockwise spirals in most of the cases will be consecutive numbers in the Fibonacci series (21, 34), (34, 55), (55, 89), or (89, 144).

Fruits like cauliflower and pineapple exhibit spiral patterns that are in the Fibonacci sequence. Normally, pineapples have three distinct series of spirals, derived from the hexagonal pattern of their scales. The number of row/scales formed in each direction is in Fibonacci numbers. The majority of pineapples have (8-13-21) rows of fruitlets i.e., scales, and a few smaller ones have (5-8-13) rows.

Note that the bottom-most leaf in a plant and also note the leaf that is almost exactly above the bottom-most leaf with many rows of leaves between them. Count the number of leaves located in between those two leaves and also count the number of turns/rotations of leaves that happen in between those two leaves. Both the resultant numbers will be in Fibonacci sequence.

The above facts assert that nature often ensures optimal arrangement of natural things through Fibonacci settings.

You may ask whether these Fibonacci ratios play the same role in the world of financial markets also as they do in nature. Yes, the Fibonacci ratios work well in financial markets also as in nature as the markets have the same mathematical base as the above-said natural phenomena. We will see in detail a little later in this chapter how and when the Fibonacci ratios are applicable to finance.

What are Fibonacci sequence and the magic ratios?

i) After 0 and 1, each number is the sum of the two previous numbers.

ii) A number in the series divided by the previous number approximates 1.618 i.e., a number in the series is approximately 1.618 times greater than the preceding number. (The inverse of 1.618 is 0.618.)

iii) A number in the series divided by the next highest number approximates 0.618. For example, 34 divided by 55 equals 0.6181, and 89 divided by 144 equals about 0.6180. (This is the basis for the 61.8% retracement.)

iv) A number in the series divided by another number that is two places higher approximates 0.382. For instance, 13 divided by 34 equals approximately 0.3823. (This is the basis for the 38.2% retracement. You may also note that $1 - 0.618 = 0.382$.)

v) A number in the series divided by the number three places higher approximates 0.236. For example, 21 divided by 89 equals about 0.236. (This is the basis for the 23.6% retracement.)
vi) When a number in the Fibonacci series is divided by a number two places prior to the given number, the result will be always 2.618 (approx).
vii) When a number in the Fibonacci series is divided by a number three places prior to the given number, the result will be always 4.236 (approx).

What are Fibonacci lines?

Fibonacci lines are horizontal lines drawn at different levels that are associated with some of the above-said Fibonacci ratios/percentages.

How to draw the Fibonacci lines?

A trendline is drawn from the low to the high i.e., from level "0" to level "100" of the last apparent trend in the stock chart. The vertical distance between these two points is divided by the major Fibonacci ratios of 23.6%, 38.2%, 50% and 61.8%. (The ratio 50% is not based on a Fibonacci ratio and it emanates from the Dow Theory that averages generally retrace to 50%). These levels are then marked and horizontal lines are drawn- the first line at 100% (the high on the chart), the second line at 61.8%, the third at 38.2%, the fourth at 23.6% and the last line at 0% (the low on the chart). In other words, a grid made up of several lines is extended from the trendline's beginning (level 0) to its end (level 100) in such a way that the distance between each of the lines is in a Fibonacci ratio.

Most of the trading softwares contain a tool that automatically draws the horizontal lines.

Using Fibonacci levels in trading financial assets

Fibonacci ratios are used in trading in two ways- Fibonacci retracements and Fibonacci extensions.

i) Fibonacci Retracements and predicting stock prices

Even when the present trend is likely to continue, the asset price usually retraces to the level at one of the ratios mentioned above viz., 61.8%, 38.2% and 23.6% and then resumes the previous trend. The levels 61.8%, 38.2% and 23.6% which lie within this range of 0 to 100 are called Fibonacci retracement levels. Fibonacci retracement levels will tell us where a pullback or correction that is occurring in the opposite direction of the main trend will come to an end and the main trend will resume. That is, Fibonacci retracement shows how much of the earlier move is likely to be retraced by the price.

After confirming the main trend, traders wait for retracement, and when they notice that the price retraces and reaches key Fibonacci level, they enter the market in the direction of main trend, and this ensures low risk.

The Fibonacci retracement levels are considered benchmarks for possible targets, trend reversals and stop loss levels. In a rising market, Fibonacci retracement lines will become support lines, and in a downtrend, these lines will work as resistance lines.

The following chart shows how Fibonacci levels become good support and resistance levels:

ii) Fibonacci extensions and predicting stock prices

The Fibonacci levels that are located after 100 viz., 123.6%, 138.2%, 161.8%, etc., are called Fibonacci extension levels. Fibonacci retracement percentages are applied to pullbacks and Fibonacci Extension percentages are applied to moves in the forward trend direction. For instance, if a security's price rises from Rs. 50 to 60 and then falls to Rs. 56, the downward move from Rs. 60 to Rs. 56 is a retracement, and if the price then resumes uptrend and rallies to 63, it is an extension.

Fibonacci extensions are major areas of value in trend direction in view of the following:

(i) Fibonacci extension lines will act as good resistance lines in an uptrend and good support lines in a downtrend.
(ii) Stop loss can be set at internal levels.
(iii) Profit booking can be at external levels.

Golden Ratio

Do you know that the number of female bees in a hive divided by the number of male bees will be always 1.618 (approx)?

Do you know that the size of the spiralling chambers of Nautilus shells increases in the ratio of 1.61?

Do you know that the length from our shoulder to finger tips divided by the length from our elbow to fingertips also works out to 1.618 (approx)?

Do you know that the distance between our head and feet divided by the distance between our belly button and feet works out to the same ratio?

Do you know that the diameters of the opposing spirals of sunflowers are in the ratio of 1.618 (approx)?

This ratio of 1.618 is literally found everywhere and is part and parcel of our life and hence is called Golden Ratio.

Two numbers are said to be in the golden ratio if the ratio of the sum of those two numbers to the larger number is equal to the ratio of the larger number to the smaller number. It can also be said that when a line is divided into two parts in such a way that the longer part divided by the smaller part is equal to the whole part divided by the longer part, the resultant ratio is the golden ratio i.e., 1.618. The Golden Ratio can also be described as one-half of the sum of 1 plus the square root of 5. The Golden Ratio is also called Phi, Golden Section, Golden Mean and Divine Proportion.

The ratios of sequential Fibonacci numbers (2/1, 3/2, 5/3, etc.) go close to the Golden Ratio. The higher the Fibonacci numbers, the closer their relationship to 1.618 as evidenced by the following:

2/1 = 2
3/2 = 1.5
5/3 = 1.666

Scientists have found that our brain likes artwork and architecture that apply the Golden Ratio to the designs, figures and structures. This proportion is found to be pleasing to our eyes as it ensures balance and harmony in the design. For instance, a rectangle with short and long sides in the ratio of 1: 1.618 will be the most appealing rectangle. Popular brands like Apple, Twitter, Toyota, Pepsi and the magazine National Geographic use the Golden Ratio in their logos. Toyota uses in their logo ovals in sizes that are in the Golden Ratio. Pepsi uses in their logo circles in sizes that are in the Golden Ratio. The magazine and TV channel National Geographic have applied the Golden Ratio in the sizes of the rectangle in their logo.

The above facts about Golden Ratio are highlighted here to show that the Golden Ratio i.e., the Fibonacci value of 1.618 is an important area of value in trading as support, resistance and take-profit levels.

Limitations of Fibonacci levels as trading tools

1) The Fibonacci retracement levels are not highly probable reversal points; they just serve as alert zones for a potential reversal. Odd levels of retracements and extensions do occur.
2) In the case of other technical indicators, we need not manually mark any value or draw any line and we can simply select the indicator from the list of indicators. But in the case of Fibonacci line, we have to determine the trend line, note the high and low values and then mark the Fibonacci values.

6. Divergences

What is divergence?

Normally, both the market price and technical indicators move in the same direction. But occasionally the market price goes one way and the Stochastic goes another way; *price reaches a new high (or new low) but the Stochastic/RSI/MACD/CCI/Accumulation Distribution Line indicator fails to follow suit* and moves in the opposite direction. That is, the market and the technical indicator are "diverging" from each other. Such divergence may be an indication that the momentum behind the current trend in price is waning, and price will soon adjust. That is, weakening downside momentum may lead to a trend reversal or a significant rally and weakening upward momentum may lead to a trend reversal or a significant decline.

Divergences will be occurring mostly after sharp movements of prices that happen after corrections.

The Stochastic, RSI, MACD, Williams %R, Money Flow Index, Commodity Channel Index, Chande Momentum Oscillator and ADL indicators are much useful to identify such divergences and trade on them.

Bullish Divergence

A bullish divergence is said to have occurred when the price of an asset continues falling while the technical indicator has started to trend higher indicating that the momentum behind the downtrend in price is losing steam and start of an uptrend is likely. In other words, a simultaneous lower low in the price and higher low in the technical indicator indicates that selling pressure in the market is decreasing, the currently prevailing downside momentum is waning, buyers are about to dominate the market and the market is likely to see a reversal of trend.

By this time, you would have understood that a bullish divergence signals a good opportunity to buy the asset at a low price.

The following chart shows a bullish divergence in a stock:

Bearish divergence

A bearish divergence is said to have happened when the price of an asset continues rising while the technical indicator has started falling. That is, price is making a higher high while the indicator is making a lower high. This indicates that buying pressure in the market is decreasing, the momentum behind the uptrend in price is losing steam and the price will soon stop rising and start falling.

Thus a bearish divergence signals a good opportunity to go short on the security.

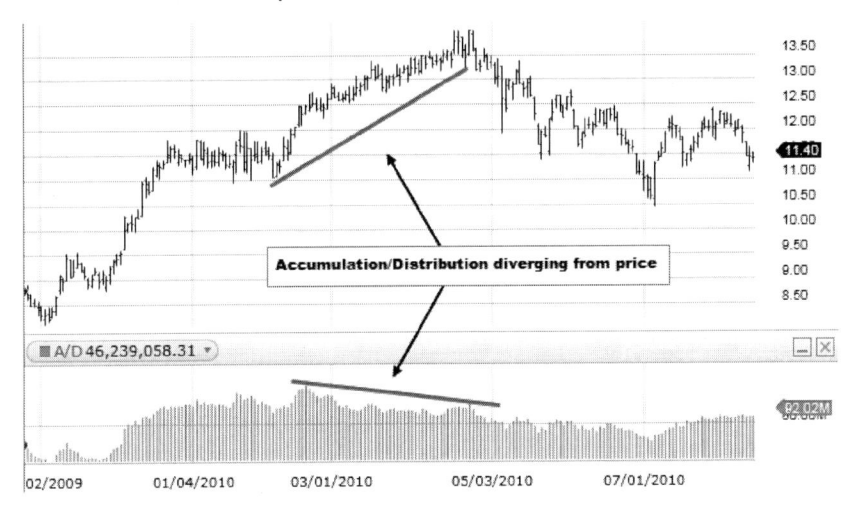

Trading divergences

Divergences are normally indications that reversal of price trend is imminent because, as said earlier, momentum changes direction before price does. *However, the ongoing price trend may not reverse immediately on the occurrence of divergence and the trend may continue for a long time as divergence is only a warning that the trend is slowing down and it does not mean that the trend will reverse. Hence the trader must wait until another technical indicator like candlestick and MACD histogram confirms a corresponding change in the price trend.*

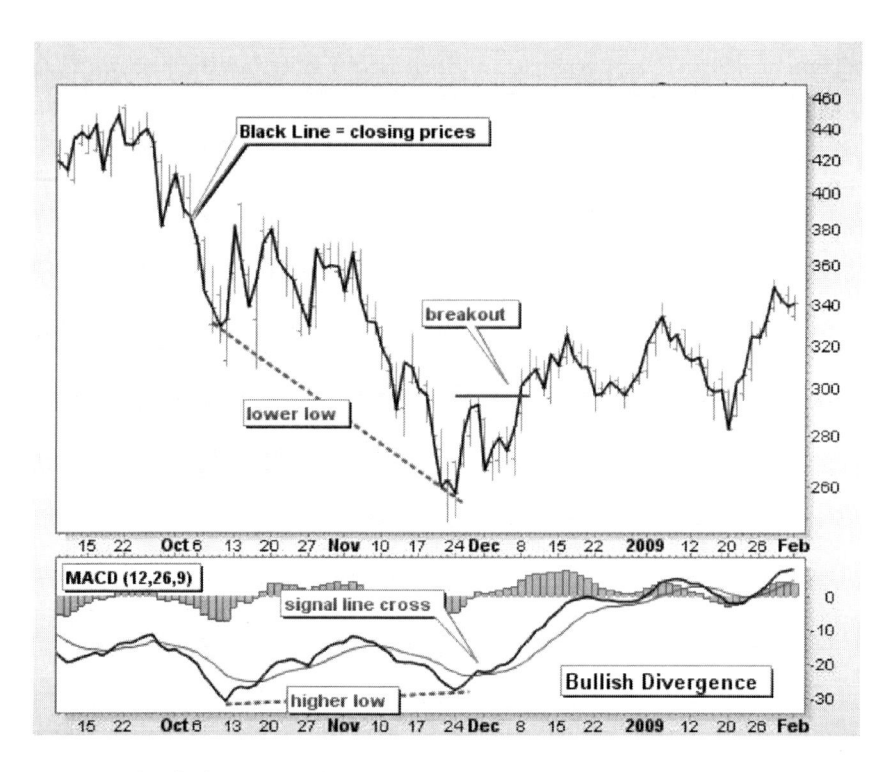

Hence don't base trades simply on divergence until an actual turnaround in price is taking place. You may take position after a corresponding change in price occurs as evidenced by a technical indicator like MACD histogram and bullish/bearish candlestick pattern.

This way of trading on the divergences between the price and RSI/MACD/Stochastic will fetch more profit as the trend reversal is noticed and trade entered early.

PART II

This part of the book explains 10 technical indicators and guides the readers how overbought and oversold conditions of securities can be identified and profitably traded.

1. Relative Strength Index (RSI)

What is RSI?

RSI calculates the speed and strength of the price trend of a stock besides the trend's direction. This is done by comparing the stock's gains and losses in prices during the specified period. That is, RSI is the ratio of average gain to average loss. In essence, RSI measures how well the stock is performing against itself by comparing the strength of its up days with the strength of its down days. Thus the indicator is a leading indicator and conveys early signs of trend reversals.

Computation of RSI

RSI is calculated using a two-step process. First, the average gains and losses are identified for the specified time period. For instance, if you want to calculate the 14-day RSI (which is the default setting in almost all the trading platforms) and suppose the stock went UP on nine days and DOWN on five days, the absolute gains (stock's closing price on a given day *minus* closing price on the previous day) on each of these nine days are added up and divided by 14 to get the average gains. Similarly, the absolute losses on each of the five days are added up and divided by 14 to get the average losses. The ratio between these values (average gains/average losses) is known as relative strength (RS). To ensure that RSI is always moving between 0 and 100, the above-said ratio is then normalized using the following formula:

RSI = 100 − 100/(1+RS)

where RS = Relative Strength = Average gains during the specified period/Average losses made during the same period.

As RSI deploys EMA, it is smoother and less erratic than many other indicators.

Be happy that you need not do the job of a mathematician and calculate the values as most of the charting softwares/trading platforms do this calculation for us.

Best setting

The default period setting of RSI is 14. This value can be increased or decreased to any number of minutes, days, weeks, months or years if the trader needs the indicator's sensitivity to be decreased or increased. For instance, a 4-day RSI is likely to reach overbought/oversold zones earlier and more often than a 14-day RSI while the latter will be more accurate and consistent. In other words, a long-period RSI will be more accurate and consistent than a shorter-period RSI indicator.

- Day traders often prefer the setting of 9–11days.
- Medium-term (swing) traders prefer the setting of 14 days.
- Long-term traders prefer the setting in the range of 20–30.

As regards overbought/oversold readings, RSI's default overbought reading is 70 and above and default oversold reading is 30 and below in most of the charting softwares. Some traders change the values as 80 and 20 respectively in the case of highly volatile securities.

Interpretation of RSI readings

1. If the RSI level of a security moves closer to 100, it implies that higher closing levels of the security are more common than lower ones and average gains significantly exceed average losses during the selected timeframe. If the level moves closer to zero, it means that lower closing levels are more common than higher closing levels and average losses significantly exceed average gains.

2. RSI reading of 70 or above indicates that the security is in overbought (or overvalued) condition and the price trend is ripe for reversal (or corrective pullback) as the high value may indicate an abnormally long run of consecutively higher prices. Similarly, a reading of 30 or below indicates that the security is in oversold (or undervalued) condition and the price trend is ripe for reversal as the low value may indicate an abnormally long run of consecutively lower prices.

3. If RSI makes new highs and higher lows, it means that the stock is in a healthy uptrend. If the RSI makes new lows and lower highs, it means that the stock is in a strong downtrend.

4. RSI provides confirmation of the primary direction of the price trend. In a strong bullish condition, the RSI rarely falls below 40 and will be mostly within the range of 50 to 80. In a strong bearish condition, the RSI rarely rises above 40.

Trading Strategies with RSI

Strategy 1: Trading overbought and oversold conditions

As the RSI value will always move between 0 and 100, the value will be 0 if the stock falls on all 14 days, and 100 if the price moves up on all the days. This implies that the RSI is much useful to ascertain the overbought/oversold condition of a stock. Generally, RSI value above

70 is considered as 'overbought zone' and value below 30 is considered as 'oversold zone'. However, some traders prefer the values 80 and 20 and some others prefer the values 75 and 25. There are also some eminent technical analysts who aver that RSI readings of 66.66 and above indicate bullish market and 33.33 and below indicate bearish market unlike the much-followed readings of 70/30 and 80/20. Traders can decide on the selection of values depending upon the inherent volatility of the concerned stock as volatile stocks may hit the overbought and oversold levels more frequently than stable stocks if the 70 and 30 levels are maintained.

One should not mistake that overbought and oversold levels are trade signals to go short or long immediately. Traders must understand that the overbought condition may continue for a very long period if there is a very strong bullish trend and oversold condition may continue for a very long period if there is a very strong bearish trend. Anticipating trend reversals immediately after the RSI crosses above 70 or crosses down 30 will lead to loss only. We should wait till the trend reversal is confirmed by subsequent candlesticks as illustrated in the chart given below:

If the RSI line reaches 70/30 and then returns towards the middle line, it is a better indication that trend reversal has taken place and it is time to initiate trade. We can buy when RSI falls below 30 but starts rising above 30 and similarly we can sell when RSI rises above 70 but starts falling below 70.

Some aggressive traders add Stochastic indicator (which will be dealt with in a separate chapter) in their charts page to know when momentum changes and price starts retracting from the extreme levels.

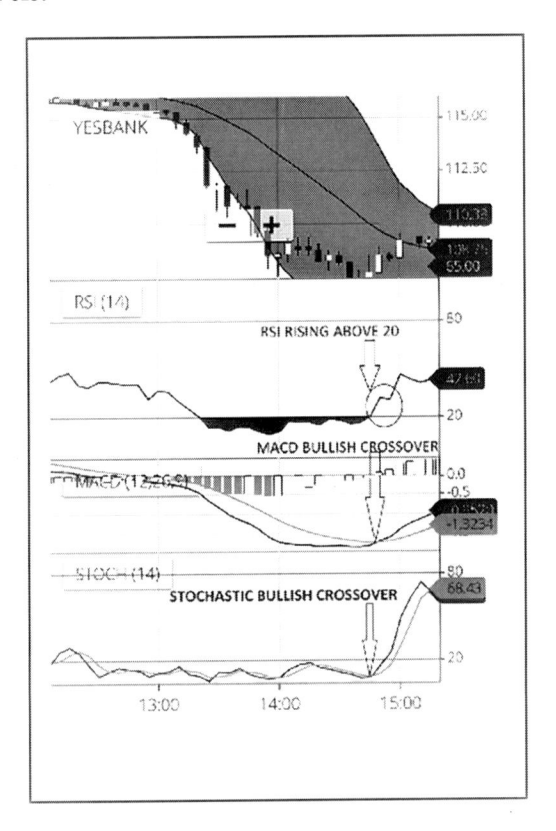

In effect, we will be acting only after trend reversal has actually begun.

Strategy 2: RSI Divergence

We have already dealt with in detail the phenomenon of divergence in a separate chapter.

When the price reaches a new high or low extreme but the RSI fails to follow suit, divergence is said to have occurred. It may be an indication that the momentum behind the current trend is waning and prices will soon adjust.

Positive divergence is said to have happened when the price of an asset continues falling while the RSI has started to trend higher. This indicates that the momentum of the downtrend in price is losing steam and an uptrend in price is likely.

Negative divergence is said to have happened when the price of the asset continues rising while the RSI has started falling. This indicates that the momentum of the uptrend in price is losing steam and the price will soon stop rising and start falling.

Since directional momentum is not in conformity with price, divergences signal a potential reversal point and hence trading divergences is a popular trading strategy.

When RSI which has been in overbought condition is now falling while price continues rising, it is a great selling opportunity.

Similarly, when RSI which has been in oversold condition is now rising while price continues falling, it is a great buying opportunity. Thus divergence is used by traders to validate the buy-sell signals of overbought and oversold conditions in view of the fact that a divergence precedes a trend reversal as price momentum expressed in the RSI values changes direction before the price does.

However, the traders should wait to take position till a corresponding change in price is observed in the form of a bullish/bearish candlestick pattern.

This way of trading on the divergences between the price and RSI will fetch more profit as the trend reversal is detected and trade entered early.

Strategy 3: RSI Middle line (Center Line) Crossing

RSI values of 70/30 indicating overbought and oversold level are not the only lines that deserve traders' attention.

Another equally important level is the middle line at 50. When the RSI crosses the middle line (i.e., RSI value of 50), it is an occurrence more important than the crossing of the values 70 and 30. Its signal that change of trend has happened is stronger than the 'overbought and oversold' signals of 70–30 lines. If the RSI value goes above 50, it means that the average gains are exceeding the average losses over the period and the market is bullish. If the RSI value goes below 50, it is a strong signal that the market is bearish; it is an indication that average losses are exceeding average gains over the period indicating that one can go in for fresh shorting or selling to cover long.

To be brief, when a centreline cross happens, it can be a good time to think about trade entry on a fresh pullback in price.

Another important thing to be noted is that the RSI value of 50 is considered by many traders as good support and resistance benchmark.

Strategy 4: Failure Swings

If we place trade orders anticipating trend reversal merely because the RSI has hit an extreme reading, it will land us in trouble because if the prevailing market trend is very strong, the trend may continue in the same direction even after the RSI hits an extreme reading. It is certain that the trend has to reverse at one point of time but how to identify that the reversal is imminent. Here comes the phenomenon "failure swing" which signals the impending reversal of trend.

What is a failure swing?

When the RSI surges above 70, falls below 70, and again rises but fails to reach the previous peak level before falling again, it is called a failure swing. Similarly, when the RSI falls below 30, rises above 30, and falls again but fails to fall to the previous low level before rising again, it is called failure swing. Occurrence of failure swing signals that the current trend is weakening and may reverse soon.

How to trade failure swings

A failure swing is used as a signal to take positions against the current trend in anticipation of a trend reversal. There are both the bearish and bullish failure swings. When a failure swing occurs during uptrend, you may go short at the level of the low swing that had been made by the indicator just before the failure swing had happened. Similarly, when a failure swing occurs during downtrend, you may go long at the level of the peak that had been formed before the occurrence of the failure swing.

Strategy 5: RSI trendline breaks

In a rising market, draw a line connecting the bottoms in the RSI line. If and when the RSI breaks this line to the downside, it will prove to be an early indication of a trend reversal to the downside. In a falling market, draw a line connecting the peaks in the RSI line. If and when the RSI breaks this line to the upside, it will prove to be an early indication of trend reversal to the upside.

Here, it must be borne in mind that a break of the trendline of RSI often precedes a break of the trendline of price.

Strategy 6: Trading the RSI values between 40 and 80 in bullish market and the values between 20 and 80 in bearish market

"Trend is your friend" is the golden rule of technical analysis. Traders are supposed to trade in the direction of the market trend only. RSI is much useful in determining the trend. For instance, RSI is usually moving between 40 and 80 and rarely falls below 40 in the case of a stock in strong uptrend. In such cases of stocks in uptrend, one is not supposed to go short. The stock may be bought at the RSI value of 40 and covered by selling when the RSI value reaches the value of 80. Stocks in strong downtrend will be mostly moving between 20 and 60, and one can consider going short if and when the RSI touches the value 60.

Strategy 7: Early signals of breakouts and breakdowns

When the RSI has broken the previous top while the price has not yet broken the previous top, it is an early signal of an impending breakout and an indication that price trend will follow the indicator's trend soon. Similarly, when the RSI has broken the previous bottom while the price has not yet broken the previous bottom and is still above the previous bottom, it is an early signal of a breakdown and an indication that some correction will take place and the price will break the previous bottom and follow the indicator's trend soon.

Strategy 8: Trading with a very short-period RSI

The 2-period RSI is extremely sensitive and will give many overbought/oversold signals. Of course, most of these overbought/oversold signals will fail because the 2-period RSI is not meant for locating significant reversals. So, when a 2-period RSI is in overbought level and it witnesses the market actually falling down, we can believe that a downtrend begins.

You may buy after the 2-period RSI falls below 5, price rises above the higher swing's high that had formed just before the RSI signal, the RSI again falls below 5 and price rises and breaks the high of a bullish candle.

You may go short if 2-period RSI goes above 95, price breaks below the lower swing's low that had formed just before the RSI signal, the 2-period RSI again rises above 95 and price falls and breaks the low of a bearish candle.

Strategy 9: Crossover of Short period RSI & Long period RSI

Select from the charts page of your trading platform a very short-period RSI, say RSI (4) and another RSI with the default setting RSI (14) in such a way that both lie on each other at the same window.

As you know, a shorter period RSI takes into account and responds to more recent price changes than a longer period RSI and hence it signals overbought and oversold conditions and trend reversals earlier than longer period RSI. Naturally, when the 4-period RSI crosses the 14-period RSI from below, it means that the recent price trend is bullish. When the 4-period RSI is in oversold zone during its upward crossover with 14-period RSI occurs, it is a reliable buy signal. Similarly, if a downward crossover of 4-period RSI with 14-period RSI occurs when the 4-period RSI is already in overbought zone, it is a reliable sell signal. When these crossovers are supported by volume and support and resistance zones, the signals will be having added strength.

Strategy 10: RSI strategies in combination with other technical indicators

Technical indicators help us identify the direction of the market, entry price level, target price and stop loss level, and they enable us to trade with confidence. However, a single indicator's signal will not be enough to take to high probability trades. Combining indicators based on different logic and basing buy-sell decisions recommended by them will enable us to avoid false signals and make more profitable trades. The buy and sell signals of any indicator must always be supported by a few other momentum indicators and trend indicators.

Here are a few such technical indicators that work well in conjunction with each other and give us high probability trades.

(i) Trading RSI with Engulfing Candlestick

When the RSI rises to the 70 line indicating overbought condition, let us wait to get a bearish engulfing candle to confirm the sell signal. After the bearish engulfing candle appears, let us go short at the open of the next trading session. Similarly, when the RSI falls to the 30-line indicating oversold condition, we will wait till a bullish engulfing candle gets formed. After the formation of such a bullish engulfing candle, we will go long at the open of the next trading session.

(ii) RSI and Moving Averages Crossover

We will take a position only when we match an RSI overbought or oversold signal with a supportive crossover of the moving averages preferably crossover of 4-period and 13-period simple moving averages or 8-period and 21-period EMAs. We will hold the position until we get the opposite signal from one of the two indicators or divergence on the chart occurs and also after the closing of a candlestick situated between the two MA lines.

(iii) RSI, MA and price line

We may buy when the price chart crosses the moving average from below and RSI enters the oversold zone, say, below 30 and then rises above 30. We may sell if the opposite of any of the above happens.

(iv) RSI and Support-Resistance zones

First, you are to note down the support and resistance levels before the market opens.

If and when RSI is below the oversold value of 30 and price is at or near a support area, you can go long on the security above the close of the succeeding bullish candle.

Similarly, If and when RSI is above the overbought level of 70 and price is at or near the resistance area, you may go for shorting below the close of the succeeding candle.

This strategy is ideal for day trading.

Trade strategies involving RSI in conjunction with technical indicators viz., MACD, Bollinger Bands and Stochastic could be found in the respective chapters of the indicators.

A word of advice: Our trading mantra is always "Trade in the direction of (strong) trend only". We should, therefore, always ignore overbought RSI signal when market is in strong uptrend and should ignore oversold RSI signal when market is in strong downtrend unless there is a strong indication of trend reversal.

2. Moving Average Convergence and Divergence (MACD)

What is MACD?

MACD stands for Moving Average Convergence Divergence. MACD is comprised of two lines derived from two moving averages of the price of a security and a histogram. It shows the changes occurring in the relationship between the two moving averages of different lengths. It is a trend following, trend capturing momentum indicator.

MACD is calculated by subtracting long-term (26-period) Exponential Moving Average (EMA) from short-term (12-period) EMA. Then a 9-day EMA of the MACD is plotted to act as a signal line and identify turns. That is, it will function as a trigger of buy and sell signals as will be seen by us in detail later.

Settings

The values "12-26-9" are the default settings of MACD charts with almost all the trading platforms. In the MACD chart with the default setting (12, 26, 9), fast MACD line is the moving average of the difference between the 12-period and 26-period moving averages and slow MACD line is the 9-period moving average of the MACD fast line. That is, MACD line is the fast line and the signal line is the slow line. Those who want more sensitivity opt for a shorter short-term MA and a longer long-term MA. MACD (6-32-6) is more sensitive than MACD (12-26-9). Those who prefer less sensitivity lengthen the moving averages. Central line and signal line crossovers occur less frequently in those less sensitive MACD charts.

Zero line is where the two moving averages (12-Day EMA and 26-Day EMA) that make up the MACD line cross each other.

And the histogram reflects the difference/gap between the MACD fast line and slow line.

Closing prices are used for all these moving averages.

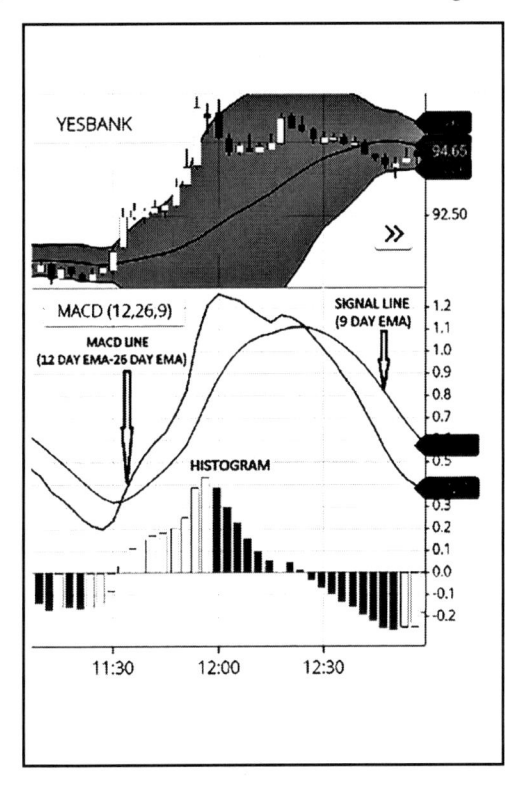

Softwares of trading platforms calculate all these values, and the calculation part is nowadays only academic in nature.

How MACD works

MACD value fluctuates above and below zero. MACD has a positive value when the 12-day EMA is above the 26-day EMA, and a negative value when the 12-day EMA is below the 26-day EMA. Positive value increases as the 12-day

EMA rises still further from the 26-day EMA implying that upward momentum is increasing still further. Negative value increases as the 12-day EMA falls still further from the 26-day EMA implying that downward momentum is increasing still further.

The moving averages used in the construction of MACD lines are exponential moving averages (EMA). As already seen by us, EMA is a type of moving average that assigns more weight and significance to the most recent data points. An exponentially moving average reacts more significantly to recent changes in price than a simple moving average (SMA) which applies an equal weight to the data of the period. A shorter period EMA assigns more weightage to recent prices than a longer period EMA. Thus MACD assigns more weight to more recent price action and thereby enables traders to ascertain whether the current trend is becoming stronger or weaker based on the slope of the MACD lines.

You can see in the above chart how the MACD is following the price trend - when price is moving up, MACD is also moving up, and when the price trend reverses, the MACD also does.

The simplest description of the trading strategy with MACD is that traders are to be prepared to buy the security when the MACD crosses the signal line from below and to go short on the security when the MACD crosses the signal line from above. An elaborate account of this strategy called signal line crossover has been given later in this chapter.

Histogram

MACD Histogram appears along with MACD and shows graphically the varying distance between the MACD line and its signal line (which is the 9-day EMA of the MACD). That is, the Histogram shows the extent to which the MACD line is above or below the signal line.

MACD Histogram = MACD Line − Signal Line.

As the difference between the two MACD lines is zero at crossovers, the histogram bar will disappear whenever crossovers take place.

Reading MACD Histogram

When the MACD line is above the signal line (which means that the market is up), the histogram will be positive and will be plotting above zero as positive values. When the MACD line is below the signal line (which means that market is down), the histogram will be negative and will be plotting below zero as negative values.

The distance between the MACD and its Signal Line i.e., the height of the histogram is in direct proportion to the strength of momentum of a stock. That is, the greater the histogram value, the greater the momentum behind the recent move. When the spread increases, the histogram becomes taller or deeper depending on its direction. When the MACD line and the signal line go nearer to each other, histogram becomes shorter. Such contraction in the histogram is a signal of weakness in momentum and is also a move towards a signal line crossover. That is, decreasing height of histogram, whether above or below the zero line, signifies that the underlying momentum is getting weaker and vice versa. Thus the histogram is able to provide an idea of the recent momentum of the trend as well as the recent direction of the trend. To put it in a nutshell, histogram above zero implies that recent movement has been higher and market is up; histogram below zero implies that the recent momentum has been down and market is down.

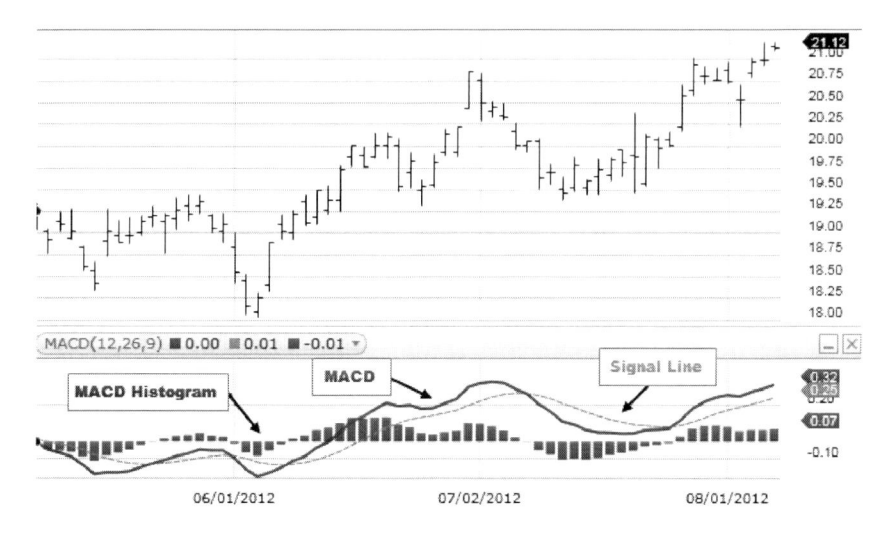

It goes without saying that zero value on the histogram indicates occurrence of a crossover of the MACD line and the signal line and it will be a major buy/sell signal.

A. Trading with MACD Histogram

A major trade signal comes when the histogram stops getting larger and starts producing a smaller bar. Such reverse movement in the histogram towards the zero line always precedes crossover signals. That is, these reverse movements are the best alert for early spotting of trade signals; when the histogram prints a smaller bar, trader looks to trade in the direction of the histogram's contraction and vice versa. In other words, we are to BUY when histogram stops falling and ticks up, and are to SHORT-SELL when histogram stops rising and ticks down.

However you must keep in mind the fact that histogram gives only an alert and it never provides a signal to go long or short; we should wait to act until the histogram crosses its zero line.

Many traders use MACD histogram as the only indicator in trading as they pin their hope mainly on price movements.

B. Trading Strategies with MACD

Traders can look for the occurrence of the following events that generate trade signals:

- Signal line crossovers
- Zero line crossovers (Central line crossovers)
- Divergences

1) Trading Signal Line Crossovers

As already seen, signal line is the 9-day EMA of the MACD Line. As a moving average of the MACD indicator, the signal line trails the MACD and makes it easier to us to spot MACD turns. When the MACD line turns up and crosses the signal line from below i.e., rises above zero, it is a bullish crossover and is a buy signal, and when the MACD line falls and crosses the signal line from above i.e., falls below zero, it is a bearish crossover and is a sell signal.

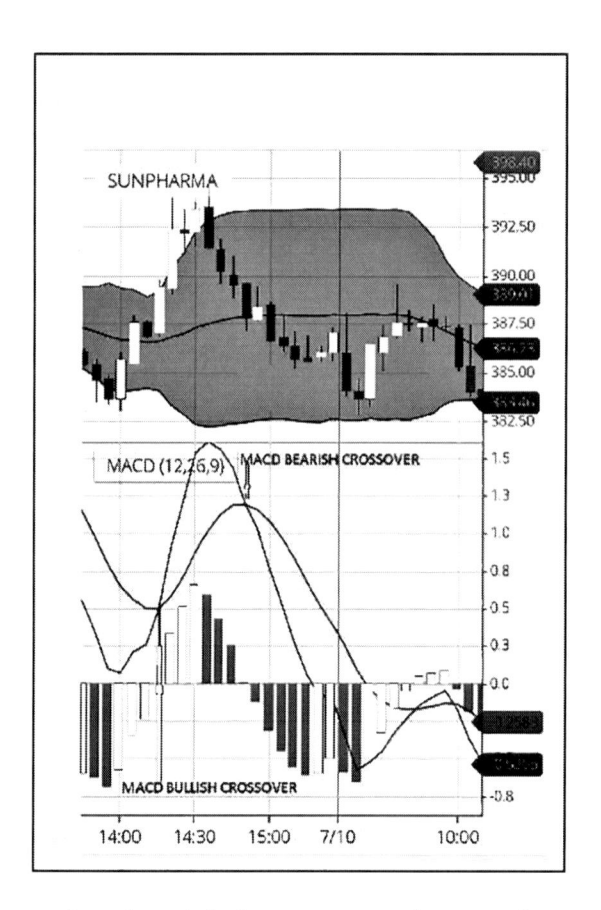

Stop loss can be placed below a recent low in the case of buy trade and above the recent high in the case of short signals.

Book profit when a crossover in the opposite direction occurs.

Fresh trades can also be taken in the direction of the new crossover.

Strength of the signal line crossover

i) It is to be kept in mind that the sharper the crossing is, the more will be the sustainability of the trend reversal as could be seen from the above chart wherein the price line falls very sharply and the MACD line also follows suit and falls sharply. Slowly crawling crossovers and the attendant trend reversals may not be sustainable and we will not, therefore, trade on those crossovers. Yes, we will trade only on sharp crossovers.

ii) Further, one must be cautious that when the MACD and the Signal line cross back and forth during a very short time because of choppy market condition, traders will be whipsawed. In range-bound markets, MACD crossover trading strategy may cause losing trades and only at trending markets will the trading be profitable.

iii) Traders must always keep in mind the universally accepted principle that long term-trend of the concerned stock must also be taken into consideration while taking any buy-sell decision as crossovers are more reliable when they are in conformity with the currently prevailing long-term trend. If the MACD crosses its signal line from below after a brief correction during a longer-term uptrend, it will be tantamount to confirmation of continuation of bullish trend, and we can go long. If the MACD crosses its signal line from above after a brief correction during a long-term downtrend, it will be tantamount to confirmation of continuation of the downtrend, and we can consider going short. It is also important to bear in mind that when the market is upward, only buy signals are to be considered for action and when the market is downward, only sell signals are to be considered for action.

iv) You are advised not to buy at a crossover that occurs much above the zero line as the farther the price is above the zero line, the closer you will be to an overbought level.

2) Trading Zero-line Crossovers (also called Central line Crossovers)

Zero line crossover (also called Central line crossover) is the next most common MACD signal. A bullish zero line crossover happens when the 12-day EMA of the stock is crossing the 26-day EMA from below i.e., when the MACD line crosses the zero line from below and turns positive indicating that a new uptrend may be emerging. A bearish zero line crossover occurs when the 12-day EMA crosses the 26-day EMA from above, ie., when the MACD line crosses the zero line from above to turn negative, indicating that a new downtrend may be emerging.

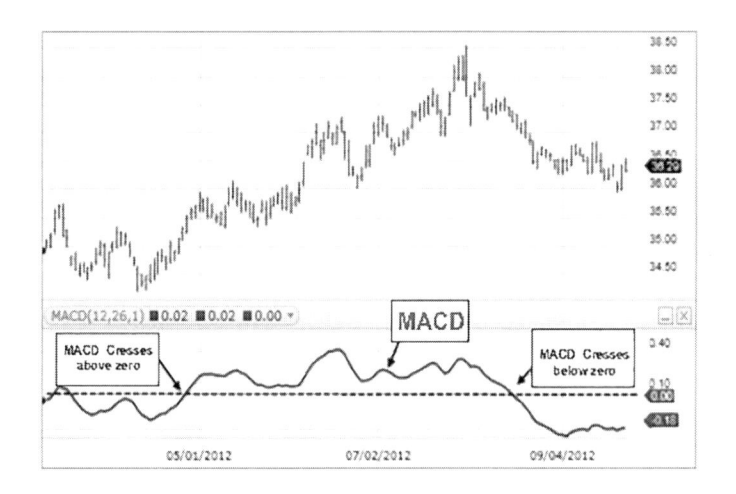

Naturally, the trading strategy is to buy when the MACD crosses the zero line from below and sell (or short sell) when the MACD line crosses the zero line from above. Hold long trades till the MACD crosses back below the zero line and hold short trades till the MACD crosses above the zero line. This strategy is very basic and doesn't have a stop loss. The trader may, therefore, place a stop loss of 1%.

Zero line crossover is mainly used to confirm trends only. When the MACD line is above zero, it confirms uptrends and supports other strategies that indicate taking long positions. When the MACD line is below zero, the MACD confirms downtrends and supports other strategies.

3) Trading divergences

We already learnt about divergences in detail in an earlier chapter.

When a stock's price is making a new high but the MACD does not make a corresponding new high, it may be an indication that the momentum behind the uptrend is waning and the prices will soon adjust. That is, when the MACD diverges from the price line, it is an indication that the momentum behind the current trend may be weakening. Weakening downside momentum may lead to a trend reversal or a significant rally and weakening upward momentum may lead to a trend reversal or a significant decline.

Naturally, a bullish divergence signals a good opportunity to buy the asset at a low price and a bearish divergence signals a good opportunity to sell the asset at a high level.

The following chart shows a bullish divergence in a stock.

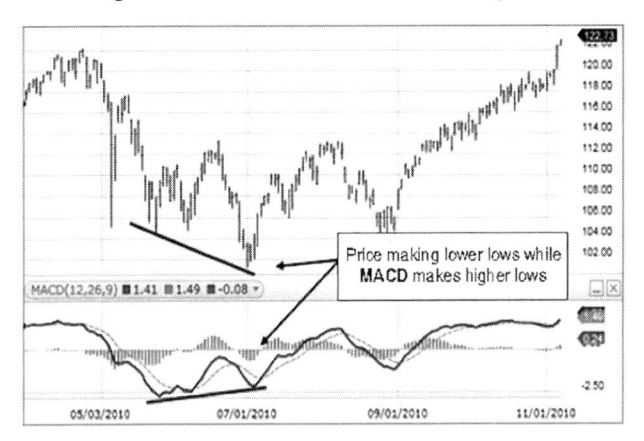

The following chart shows a bearish divergence in a stock.

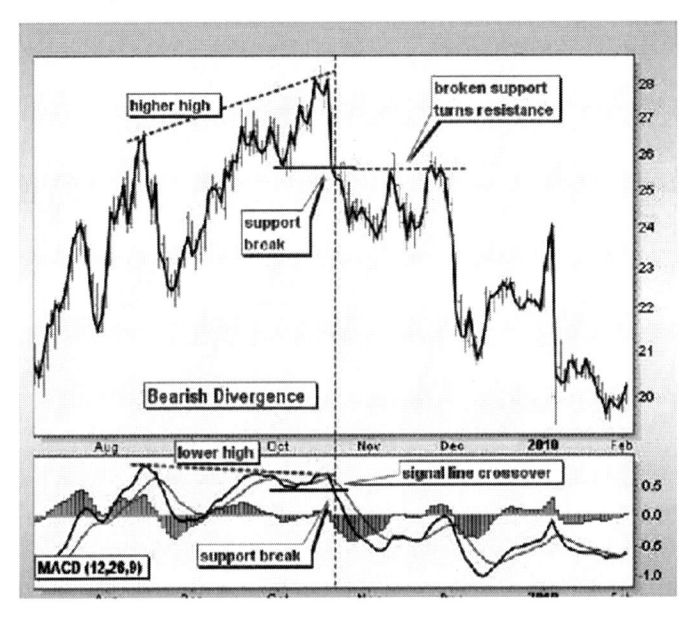

When RSI/Stochastics/MACD which has been in overbought zone is now falling while price continues rising, it is a great selling opportunity. Similarly, when RSI/Stochastic/MACD which has been in oversold condition is now rising while price continues falling, it is a great buying opportunity. Thus divergence is used by traders to validate the buy-sell signals of overbought and oversold conditions in view of the fact that a divergence precedes a trend reversal as price momentum expressed in the RSI values changes direction before the price does.

This way of trading on the divergences between the price and technical indicator like MACD will fetch more profit as the trend reversal is noticed and trade entered early.

However, divergence is only a warning that the trend has slowed down and it does not mean that price trend will reverse; a stock can continue to rise or fall for a long time even when a bearish/bullish divergence has occurred as could be seen from the following chart.

Hence don't base trades simply on divergence until an actual turnaround in price is taking place. You may take position after the occurrence of a corresponding change in price as evidenced by a price action indicator like bullish/bearish candlestick pattern.

C. Trading MACD in conjunction with other indicators

As MACD has no fixed minima-maxima range, it does not indicate exact overbought and oversold readings. Hence the MACD is better used in conjunction with indicators like RSI and Stochastic to confirm the direction of the current trend and its strength and also to identify divergences.

i) MACD and RSI

You can go long when the RSI gives oversold signal and MACD gives bullish signal line crossover. Similarly, you can go short when the RSI gives overbought signal and the MACD gives bearish signal line crossover. You may close the position even if one of the indicators gives exit signal.

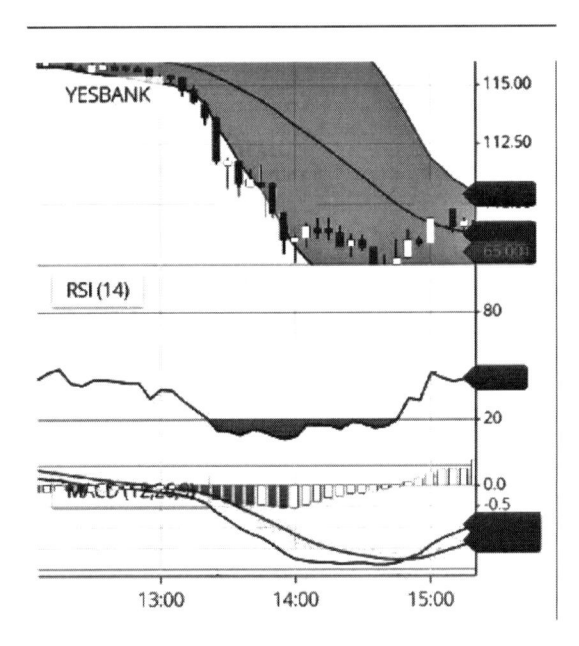

Traders are to enter into market when BOTH the RSI and MACD give an overbought/oversold signals and the position shall be closed even if one of the indicators gives exit signal.

ii) MACD + MFI

If the MFI gives an overbought signal, we will go short after a bearish MACD crossover occurs. Similarly, if the MFI gives a oversold signal, we will go long after a bullish MACD crossover occurs. We will exit when the MACD crossover in the other direction occurs.

iii) MACD + MA + RSI

MACD indicator being an oscillator, a trend-following indicator will be a good pair to the former. Moving Average which is a trend indicator fits in well in this category and works as a good complementary tool to MACD.

The trade signals that can be expected from the combo will be as follows:

1) Buy if the price line crosses the MA from above and the histogram also crosses its average in the same direction i.e., in the upward direction.
2) Sell if price line crosses the moving average from below and the histogram crosses its average in the same direction.

As MA and MACD filter each other's signals, false signals are minimal. They will show to us the current trend along which we are supposed to trade and thereby we will be safeguarded from trading in the wrong direction. If RSI also joins the party, its overbought and oversold values will show to us ideal entry points and thereby will ensure timely entry to trade and harvesting of maximum profit.

Limitation

MACD crossover trading strategy may cause losing trades in range-bound market and only at trending markets will the trading be profitable.

3. Bollinger Bands

"Bollinger Bands" is a must-have technical analysis tool for traders in stocks, currencies and commodities to gain insight into the price movement and volatility of assets.

For charting the Bollinger Bands, three different lines are drawn-one line is the stock's 20-period simple moving average, another line is drawn above the 20-period simple moving average and a third line is drawn below the 20-period simple moving average.

The following are the default settings for Bollinger Bands in almost all the trading platforms:

> Middle band and is a 20-days SMA of the closing prices. This is calculated by adding up the closing prices of the asset for 20 consecutive days and dividing the value by 20.
>
> Upper band is the Middle band plus 2 standard deviation.
>
> Lower band is the Middle band minus 2 standard deviation.

These three lines form an envelope and show a band (a volatility range) within which the particular stock's price is normally moving. (Standard Deviation is a statistical tool that measures volatility; here it shows the extent to which the stock price normally deviates from the average. When the market has high price fluctuation, the bands widen, and when the market becomes less volatile, the bands contract.

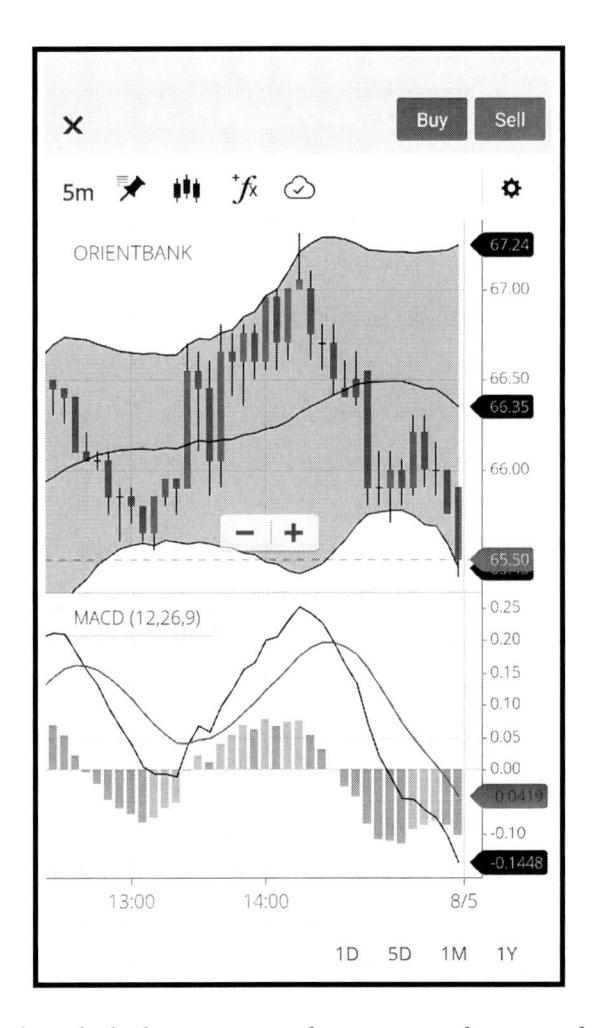

Bollinger bands help us assess how strongly a stock is rising or falling and when the stock is potentially losing strength or reversing. This information can be used to take right trading decisions.

The main advantage of this indicator is that it can be used in both trending and ranging markets.

How this indicator works

As already said, Standard Deviation is a measure of volatility and here it indicates volatility around the price of a security.

Studies have revealed that normally price will be within the range of 1 standard deviation 68% of the time and will be within the range of 2 standard deviations 95% of the time.

When the price is rising and goes near or crosses the upper band from below, it is considered overbought, and theoretically, it could be a good exit point. When price falls below the lower band, it is considered oversold and theoretically, it could be a good entry point.

Best settings

Day traders prefer 10-day SMA and bands at 1.5 standard deviations.

Traders with medium-term trade in mind prefer 20-day SMA and bands at 2 standard deviations.

Traders with long-term trade in mind go in for 50-day SMA and bands at 2.5 standard deviations.

Interpreting Bollinger Bands' body language i.e., direction, expansion and contraction

i) If both the outer bands widen from the middle band, it means that market becomes more volatile, the existing trend may come to an end and reversal of the trend may happen. If both the bands start narrowing, it means that momentum behind that trend is waning, market becomes less volatile and a trending move may soon begin and a sharp price change (break out) in either direction can be expected.

ii) If the price breaks the upper band from below and both upper & lower bands are widening, then more up move is highly probable. If the price breaks the lower band from above and both upper and lower bands are widening, it is highly likely that the price will go further down.

iii) If price breaks the upper band from below but both the bands are not widening, it is probably a false signal of break out.

iv) When the price is at the top or bottom, look at the shape of the band. If it is curving inward on both sides, don't trade; if it is opening up wide on both sides, take a trade depending on which band the price is at.

v) When price is above the middle band and is moving towards the upper band, that signals a bullish market. When the price is below the middle band and is moving towards the lower band, that signals a bearish market.

vi) If price stays firmly above the upper band or rises steadily above the upper band, it indicates that the uptrend is so strong that trend reversal is not imminent. Likewise, if price stays firmly below the lower band or declines steadily below the lower band, it indicates that the downtrend is so strong that trend reversal is not imminent. However, in the above cases, if price immediately retracts to the inside of the Bollinger Bands, then the proclaimed trend strength is considered to be waning.

Trading Bollinger Bands

1) The upper and lower bands indicate probable highs and lows respectively i.e., they provide resistance and support levels respectively.

2) When price makes a strong up move from the lower band, crosses middle line and continues the uptrend, the upper band can be a good price target. Similarly, prices falling

from the upper band and crossing down the middle band will find the lower band as a good price target.

3) If price stays above the middle band and touches the upper band often, it means that the stock is strong and can be bought with the upper band as the price target.

4) If a stock which is in an uptrend and is above the middle line ever touches the lower band, it means that the stock's uptrend is losing strength and a trend reversal may be in the offing. We can go short with the lower band as the price target.

5) In a strong uptrend, price usually fluctuates between the middle line and the upper band. In such a condition, a crossing below the middle line warns of a trend reversal to the downside. You can consider trading this reversal with support and resistance in place.

6) Buy when the lower band begins an uptrend and a bullish reversal candlestick pattern (green colour) appears. Sell when the upper band begins a downtrend and a bearish candlestick pattern (red colour) appears. However, it will be safer if any such buy decision is taken only if RSI goes below 30% indicating oversold market and sell decision may be taken only if RSI goes above 70% indicating overbought market.

7) **Trading overbought/oversold condition:** The most common use of Bollinger Bands is to identify overbought/oversold condition of a security. When the price of the security is near the lower band or continually touches the lower band or breaks below the lower band, it means that price has probably fallen too much i.e., oversold and is likely to bounce. Similarly, when the price of the security is near the upper band or continually touches the upper band or breaks above the upper band, it means that the security is probably overbought and is expensive and a pullback is likely.

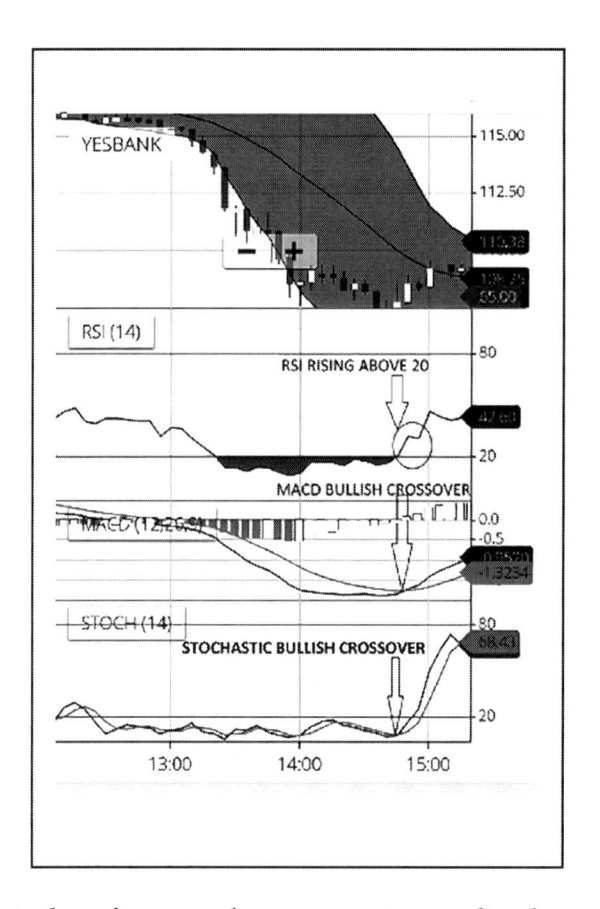

However, it doesn't mean that you can immediately enter into a trade immediately just because the stock seems to be cheap or expensive because, in trending markets, the market can remain "cheap" or "expensive" for an unexpectedly long period of time. That is, Bollinger Bands don't always give accurate buy and sell signals as the price may remain above the upper band or below the lower band for a long time and the trader will constantly be placing trades on the wrong side of the move. How can we then find out when the price reverts to the mean? You must wait for a change in the direction of the price line. It is for this purpose that the trader should take the support of additional technical analysis tools like MACD, RSI, Support, Resistance and Candlestick patterns as detailed later in this chapter.

In the above chart, you can see that prices continue to fall and Bollinger Band continues to remain in oversold condition for a long period and reversal of the downtrend begins as soon as other technical indicators signal.

8) **Multiple Bands Strategy:** Generate two sets of Bollinger Bands, one set using the parameter of "1 standard deviation" and the other using the usual setting of "2 standard deviation". Let us call them BB1 and BB2 respectively. Now you can perceive price action in an entirely different way.

The following chart depicts how multiple bands appear:

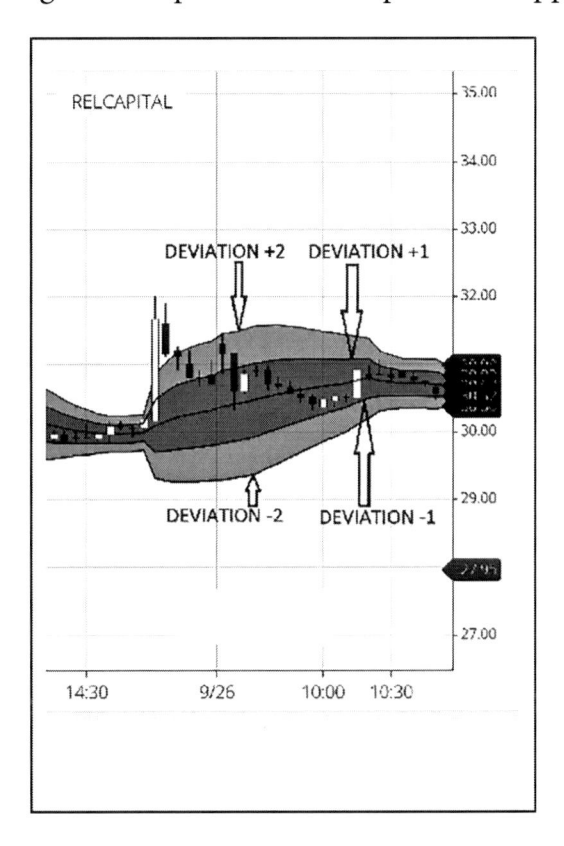

- Whenever price moves between the upper Bollinger Bands +1 SD and +2 SD away from mean, the trend is up and we can define that channel as the buy zone. If the price channel is within Bollinger Bands −1 SD and −2 SD, it is in the sell zone.

- If and when a candlestick closes above the +1 SD and the previous two candlesticks had closed below that, it is a buy opportunity and you can buy at the close of the current candlestick. You can set stop loss at below the recent candle's low.
- If a candlestick closes below the −1 SD and the previous two candles had closed above that −1 SD, it is an opportunity to go short. Go short and set stop loss at above the high of the recently closed candle.
- If the price is between +1 SD and −1 SD, it means that trend is absent or weak, and you avoid trading.

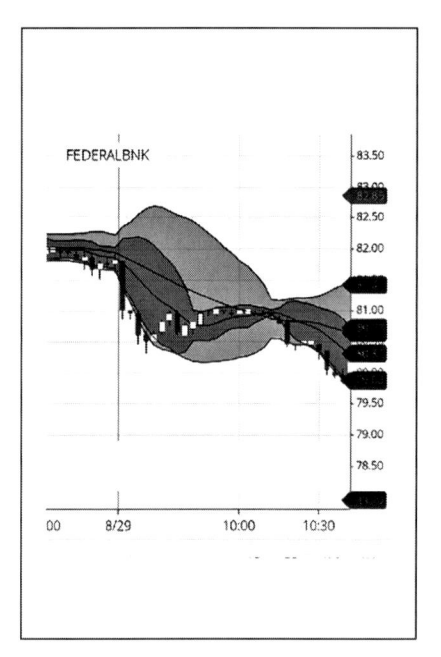

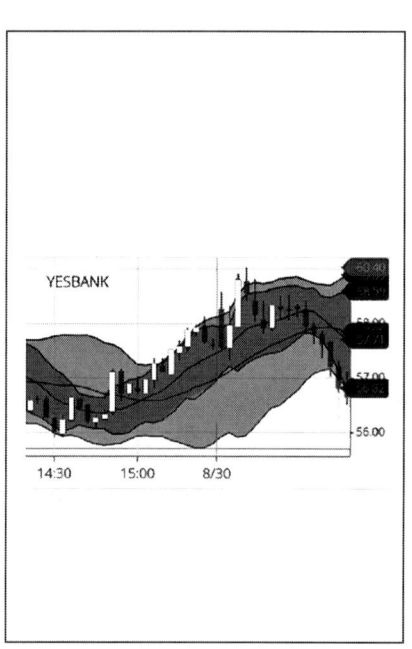

You can also observe from the above two charts that every change in the direction of price line is clearly and promptly reflected by BB1's bands by its changing direction. Yes, the BB1 reflects the price trend reversal earlier than the BB2 and with more assertiveness by meticulously changing its direction.

9) **Trading the concept of Mean Reversion:** Whenever the price of an asset gets too far away from the middle line,

the price generally tends to revert to the middle band as could be seen from the following chart. This tendency is called mean reversion. In an ideal situation, the trader can buy (or sell) as soon as the price touches the lower (or upper band) because of this mean reversion tendency. But any buy-sell decision can be taken only with the support of other indicators like MACD and Stochastics.

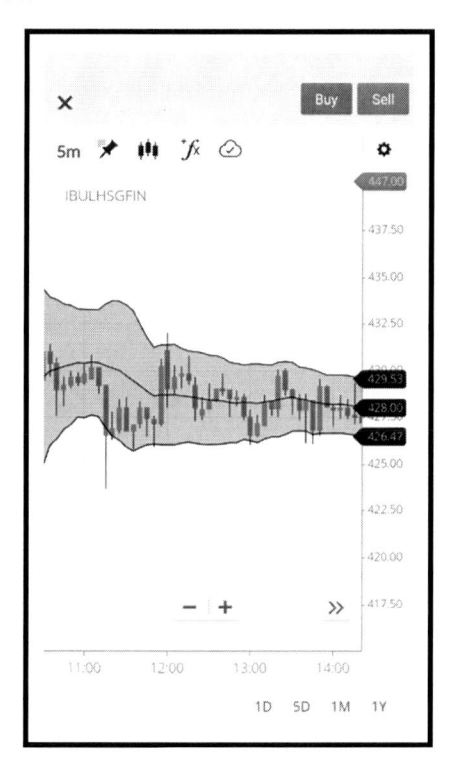

10) **Trading Breakout After Bollinger Bands Squeeze:** When the bands contract and come close to each other, a squeeze is said to have happened. The squeeze i.e., contraction of the bands is an indication that the market is undergoing low volatility. Such periods of low volatility will always be followed by periods of high volatility involving big moves in either upward direction or downward direction. That is, every squeeze would be followed by a breakout. As about 85% of price action is taking place between the upper and

lower bands, any breakout above or below the bands is a major event warranting traders' attention. Yes, it is correct. But will the breakout after squeeze be rising of price or falling of price? If the price candle breaks through the upper band, it implies a bullish breakout and the trader is to buy the stock; if the price breaks the lower band, it implies a bearish breakout and the trader is to short-sell the stock.

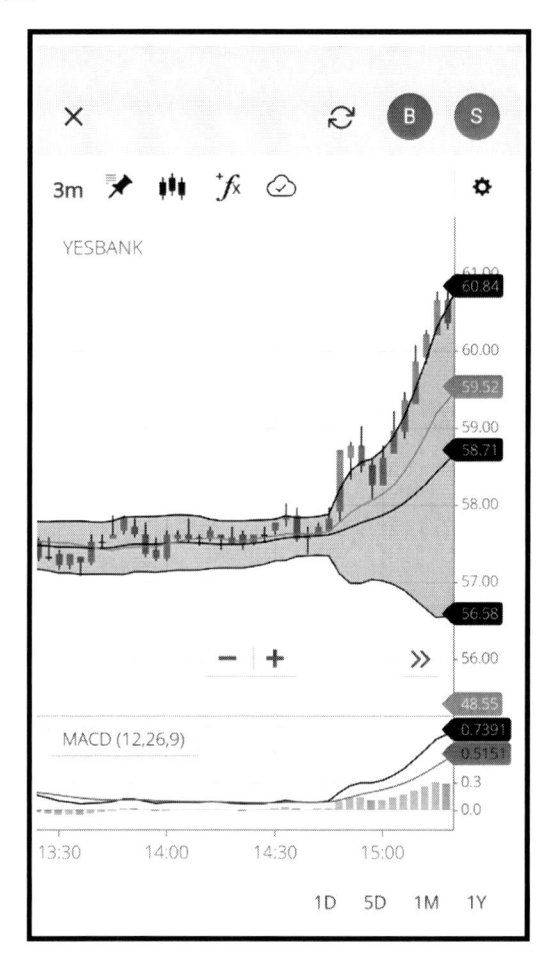

It is also important to understand that the longer the period of squeeze, the stronger the breakout and the more the trading opportunities.

In essence, in ranging markets, we are to look out for price returning to the mean and in trending markets, we are to trade on Bollinger Squeeze.

11) **Confluence of Bollinger Bands with other technical indicators:** Bollinger Bands don't always give accurate buy and sell signals as the price may remain above the upper band or below the lower band for a long time and the trader will constantly be placing trades on the wrong side of the move. How can we find out when the price is going to revert to the mean? For this purpose, the trader should take the support of technical analysis tools like MACD, RSI, Support, Resistance and Candlestick patterns.

For instance, if the security's price crosses the Bollinger Band's upper band from below and simultaneously RSI crosses 70 from below, it means that the security is overbought and you can go short when either of them starts falling. If the price crosses the lower Bollinger Band from above and RSI falls below 30, it means that the security is oversold and we can consider going long when either of them starts rising.

Similarly, if the security's price crosses the Bollinger Band's upper band from below and the upper band coincides with a resistance level, you should anticipate a bearish trend reversal. If the security's price crosses the Bollinger Band's lower band from above and the lower band coincides with a support level, you can anticipate a bullish trend reversal.

A piece of advice: Trade with the trend. You should look at the overall direction of price and then consider only those trade signals that align the trade with the overall trend. For example, if the trend is down, you should take only short positions when the upper band is tagged. The lower band can still be used as an exit, if desired, but a new long position is not to be opened as that would mean going against the trend.

4. Stochastic Oscillator

Introduction

Stochastic indicator is a momentum indicator like MACD and RSI, and is useful to determine how strong or weak the current trend is, whether an asset is overbought/oversold and where the current trend might be ending. It does it by measuring the momentum in the market trend by comparing the stock's closing price to its price range over a certain period. It is to be noted that RSI is computed using average gains and losses.

The construction of the indicator is based on the premise that when a security's price trends upwards, its closing price will tend to trade at the high end of the day's range and when a stock trends downwards, its closing price will trend to trade at the low and hence closing prices are more important in predicting oversold and overbought conditions in the market. In other words, securities tend to close near their highs in uptrends and near their lows in downtrends. Based on this assumption, the Stochastic indicator gives the traders the best trade signals.

Momentum changes its direction before price changes its direction (since momentum change is the cause and price change is the effect). Hence the stochastic indicator works as a leading indicator and helps traders enter into trade at the very beginning of the trend.

Calculation of the stochastic indicator

Stochastic oscillator usually consists of two lines plotted on a separate chart – one line is the Stochastic indicator's current value and the other is its 3-day SMA which is to act as a signal line. The former is called %K and the latter is called %D. When these two lines meet, the occurrence is considered as a signal of impending trend reversal since momentum precedes price.

The stochastic oscillator is calculated by subtracting the period's low from the current closing price, dividing by the total range of the period and then multiplying by 100. (Like RSI, the default setting for the stochastic indicator is also 14 periods which means that the %K line uses the most recent closing price and the highest high and the lowest low over the last 14 periods). This is given below in the format of a formula:

%K = (Most Recent Close – Lowest Low of the previous 14 trading sessions)/(Highest High during the previous 14 trading sessions – Lowest Low of the previous 14 trading sessions) × 100

The following is an example of calculation of the Stochastic indicator:

If the session's high is Rs. 100, low is Rs. 65 and the current close is Rs. 95, the Stochastic reading for the current session will be

(95−65)/(100−65) × 100 = (30/35) × 100 = 85.7%

The line %K is sometimes referred to as the slow stochastic indicator and the line %D as the fast stochastic indicator.

However, you can heave a sigh of relief to be told that you need not strain in making these calculations as today's charting softwares do all the calculations and readily show to you the readings.

The Best Settings

Some traders think that different trading styles like day trading, swing trading, scalping trading and positional trading need different stochastic settings. Day traders choose low-period settings like 5-3-3 which gives earlier signals with more overbought and oversold readings, and long-term players choose long-period settings like 21-14-14 which provide fewer overbought and oversold readings. But don't get entangled in quixotic acts and rest assured that the default setting is the best for most of the occasions. The default setting of stochastics is 14 periods as in the case of RSI.

Interpreting the readings of the Stochastic indicator

1) A high stochastic value indicates that upward momentum is strong, price is very strong over the period and recent prices are rising. A low stochastic value indicates that the momentum to the downside is strong.
2) The stochastic centreline (value 50) shows whether the prevailing trend has momentum or not. If the stochastic reading is above 50 and continues rising, the trend is said to have upward momentum, and if the stochastic reading is below 50 and continues falling, the trend is said to have downward momentum.
3) When prices move away from these extremes towards the middle of the price range, it is interpreted as a sign of the exhaustion of momentum and the possibility of a trend reversal.
4) Readings above 80 occur when the security is trading near the top of the high-low range. Readings below 20 indicate that the security is trading near the low end of the high-low range. That is, if the reading rises above 80, the asset is considered to be on the verge of being overbought and a downtrend is likely to follow. If the %K line drops below 20, the asset would be considered oversold, and an uptrend is likely to follow.
5) *When the %K-line crosses the signal line i.e., %D-line from below, it indicates that the current closing price is closer to the highest high of the specified time period than it has been in the earlier sessions.* This is viewed as a signal of impending bullish trend reversal and one can go for buying provided the %K value is below 80. (This is so because if the value is above 80, it implies that the stock is already in overbought condition and it will not be profitable to buy at that level.)

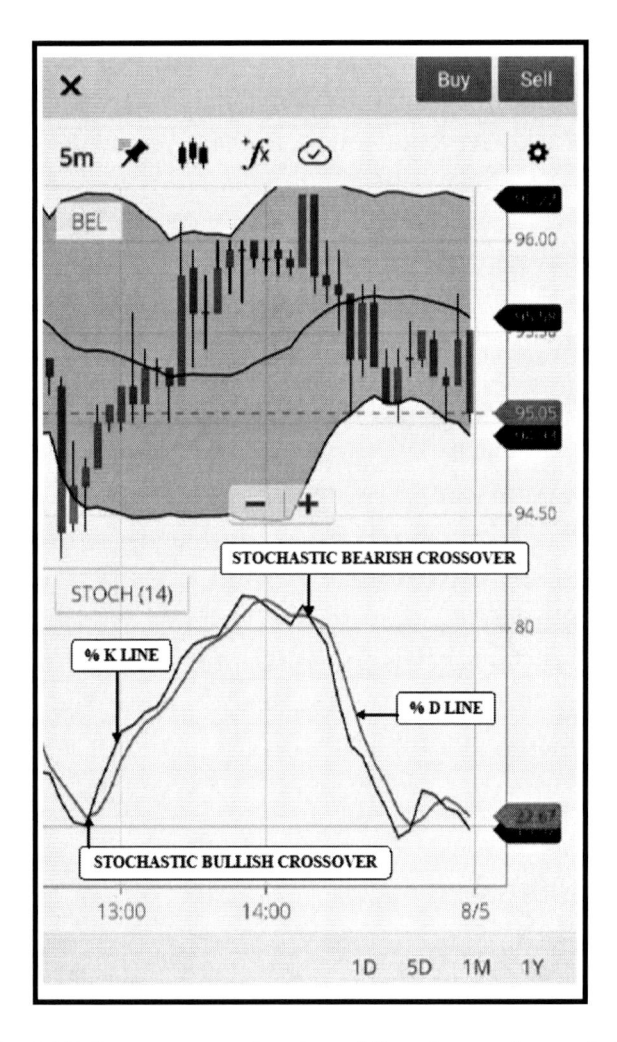

When the %K-line crosses the signal line from above, it indicates that the current closing price is closer to the lowest low of the specified time period than it has been in the earlier sessions. This is viewed as a signal of impending bearish trend reversal and as a selling signal provided the values are above 20.

Trading the stochastic oscillator

1) If %K is near 100 and has just started declining, the stock should be sold before the value falls below 80.
2) Trading overbought and oversold conditions with Stochastic oscillator

As said earlier, the Stochastic Oscillator is range-bound i.e., within a range of 0 to 100 and hence is useful for identifying overbought and oversold levels that may lead to reversal of trends. Many traders consider Stochastic readings over 80 as overbought level and that a downtrend is likely and readings under 20 as oversold level and an uptrend is likely.

However, these are not always a reliable indication of imminent reversal as very strong trends can remain in overbought or oversold conditions for prolonged periods. Trading with the hope that Stochastic's extreme readings will lead to early trend reversals will actually lead to erosion of our funds position as the Stochastic indicator shows momentum only and not oversold or overbought prices and those extremes are not always indicative of imminent trend reversal. The extreme readings i.e., more than 80 and less than 20 are telling traders that the market is probably in a strong trend and the trend will probably continue unless and until a trigger happens and changes the ongoing momentum.

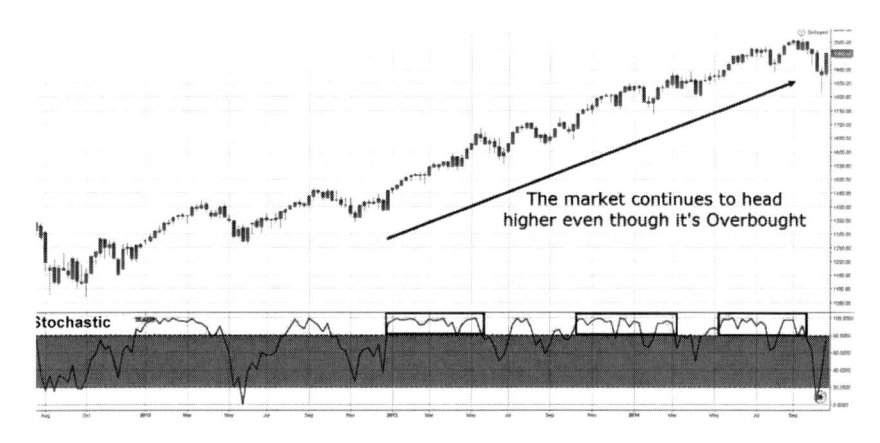

Closing levels that are consistently near the bottom of the range do indicate sustained selling pressure and closing levels that are consistently near the top of the range do indicate sustained buying pressure, and what we can understand is that a high extreme has a high probability of prices falling and a low extreme has a high probability of prices rising.

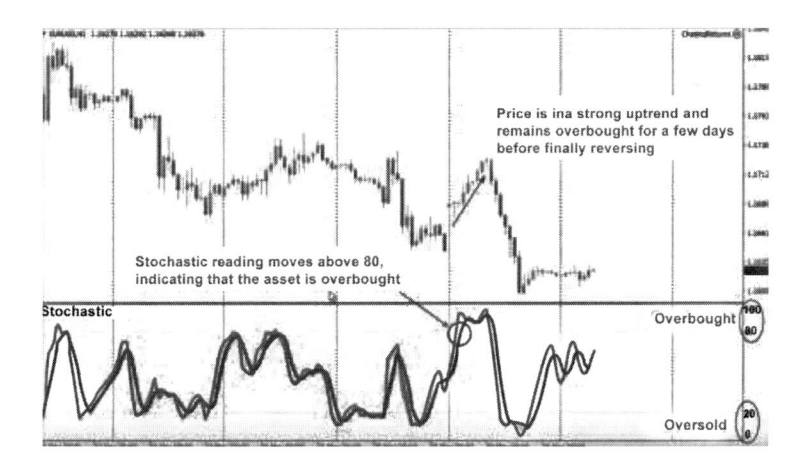

You must always, therefore, identify the bigger trend of the market and trade in the direction of the trend – look for oversold readings during strong uptrends and overbought readings during strong downtrends.

How to trade oversold conditions during an overall uptrend following the oft-repeated principle of trading in the direction of the overall trend is demonstrated in the following chart:

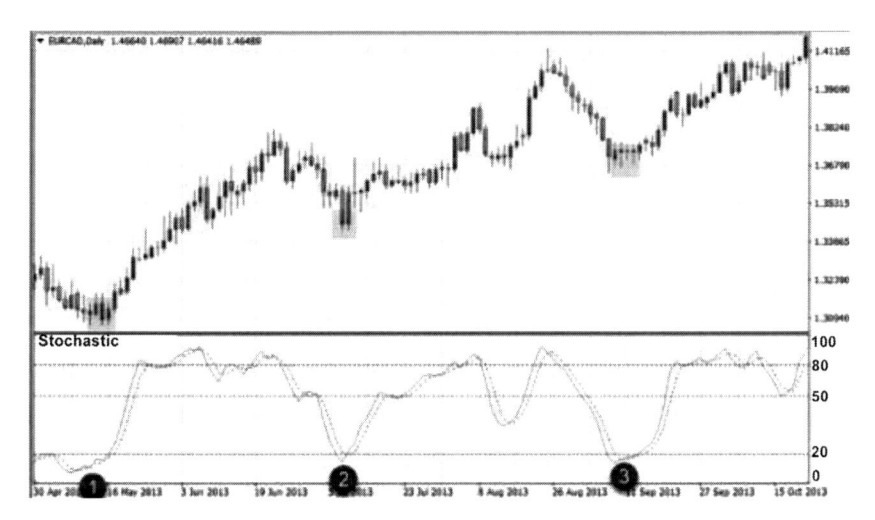

The stock is in oversold conditions at the price levels indicated by arrows while the stock is in an overall uptrend. Oversold conditions happen during up trends because of corrections.

These occasions are good opportunities to go long. When to enter? Enter when the %K line crosses the %D line (signal line) from below. Similarly, you can go short when the stock is in overbought zone and the %K line crosses the %d line from above.

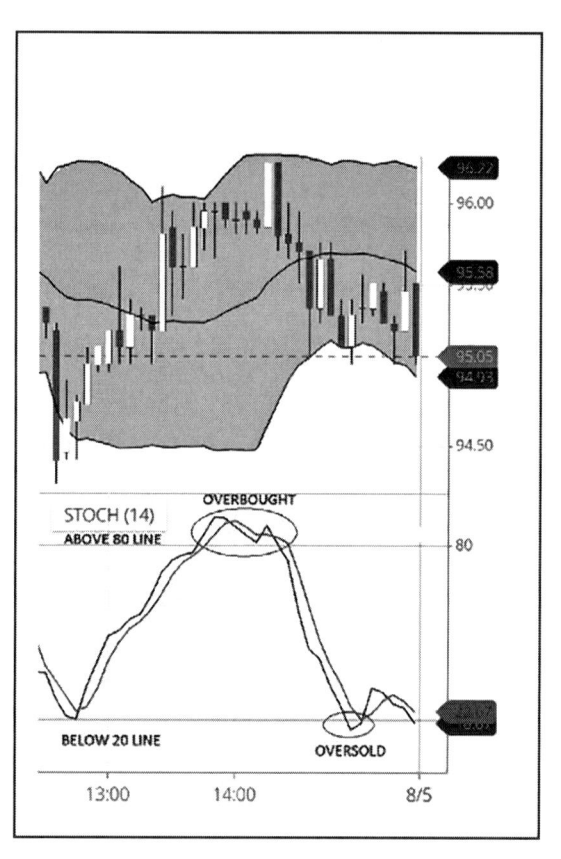

3) Trading divergences

Normally, both the market price and technical indicators move in the same direction. But occasionally they don't make simultaneously higher highs or lower lows; the market price goes one way and the Stochastic goes another way. *Price reaches a new high or new low but the stochastic indicator fails to follow suit* i.e., they are "diverging" one from another. The stochastic indicator is mainly used to identify such divergences and trade on them.

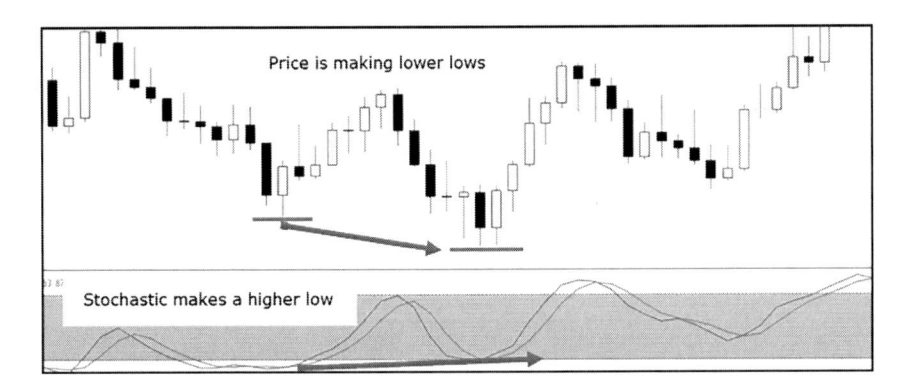

A bullish divergence is said to have formed when the price makes a lower low while the stochastic oscillator makes a higher low which is taken as an indication that the momentum behind the downward momentum is waning and a bullish reversal is likely.

A bearish divergence is said to have formed when the price makes a higher high, while the stochastic oscillator makes a lower high which is taken as an indication that the momentum behind the rising prices is waning and the price will soon adjust.

These divergences are normally indications that a price trend reversal is imminent because, as said earlier, momentum changes direction before price does and hence bullish and bearish divergences in the Stochastic Oscillator and price can be considered as a prelude to trend reversals.

Thus Stochastic divergences provide traders profitable trading opportunities.

However, the ongoing price trend may not reverse immediately on the occurrence of divergence and may continue for a while as could be seen from the following chart and hence the trader must wait until a price action indicator like candlestick and MACD histogram confirms a corresponding change in the price trend.

Bullish divergence that failed

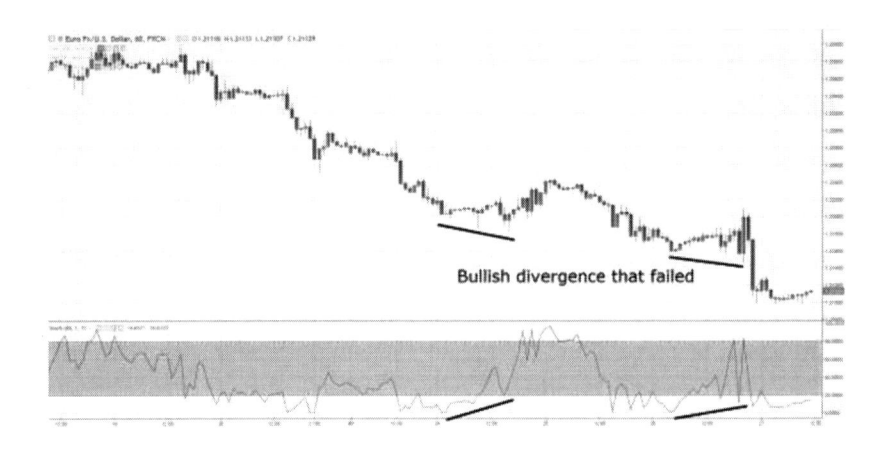

4) Confluence of indicators

Indicators help us identify the direction of the market, entry price level, target price and stop loss level and they enable us to trade with confidence. However, a single indicator's signal will not be enough to take high probability trade signals. Combining indicators based on different logic and basing buy-sell decisions on their recommendations will enable us to avoid false signals and make more profitable trades.

Here are a few such technical indicators that work well in conjunction with each other and give us high probability trades.

(i) Stochastics and Moving Averages' crossover

When a faster MA (i.e., short period MA) crosses a slower MA (i.e., longer period MA) from below, it means that an uptrend is in place and we can consider buying. However, we will consult Stochastic and confirm that the latter also gives the same signal as the MA crossover.

(ii) Stochastic, Price line and MA

Moving Averages are good at ascertaining market trends, and we will be trading based on their signals as our strategy is to trade always in the direction of market trend. We will consider buying if price is above the long-period Moving Average like 200-day moving average and Stochastic is oversold i.e., below the level 30 so that false buy signal is eliminated. Likewise, if price is below MA, we can consider going short if Stochastic is overbought i.e., above the level 70.

(iii) Stochastic and Pivot Points

Pivot Points is a popular indicator that shows multiple support and resistance lines. These lines can provide definitive price zones where traders can watch out for stochastic trade signals. A high probability trade signal is delivered when there is such confluence between Stochastic and pivot points. Note down the support and resistance levels as shown by pivot points as areas of value. Now Stochastic Indicator will provide you entry trigger. For instance, a high-quality long trade can be entered when market is in uptrend and stochastic crosses above 30 on a Pivot Points support line. Similarly, we will go short when market is in a downtrend and Stochastic crosses below 70 on a Pivot Points resistance line.

(iv) Stochastics and RSI

Though both the Stochastic and RSI are momentum indicators, they determine overbought and oversold levels by different means. To identify overbought and oversold levels, Stochastic oscillator proceeds on the assumption that securities tend to close near their highs in uptrends and near their lows in downtrends while RSI determines the overbought and oversold conditions by measuring the velocity of price movements. As RSI can remain in overbought and oversold conditions for a prolonged period and price can remain high/low for quite a while, consulting the Stochastic values will enable us to know when the momentum changes and price starts retreating from the oversold and overbought zones. When both the indicators give the same buy-sell recommendation, we can expect a high probability trade.

(v) Stochastic, RSI and Moving Average

This combo of indicators gives high probability trade signals.

First, enable the following indicators in the charts page of your trading software:

1) 14-period RSI with readings of 70 and 30 as overbought and oversold levels.
2) 14-period Stochastics with readings of 80 and 20 as overbought and oversold levels.
3) 10-period Simple Moving Average.

BUY when

- both RSI and Stochastic come out of oversold zones and
- price line crosses the SMA line from below.

SHORT-SELL when

- both RSI and Stochastic come out of overbought zones and
- price line crosses the SMA line from above.

It is important that all the three requisite signals should be received within the three succeeding candles, and if not, no trade is to be entered into.

When the RSI enters the opposite zone, the position is to be closed.

(vi) Stochastic crossover and MACD crossover

MACD indicator is useful to determine the trend as it gives us a clear signal when the trend changes; the stochastic indicator is useful to determine entry and exit points.

If a bullish crossover of the MACD line and the signal line occurs (when histogram value becomes zero), it is a buy signal. If the stochastic bullish crossover also occurs i.e., if the %K line crosses the %D line from below, it confirms the buy signal. When both the above occur, BUY. When the opposite occurs, SELL.

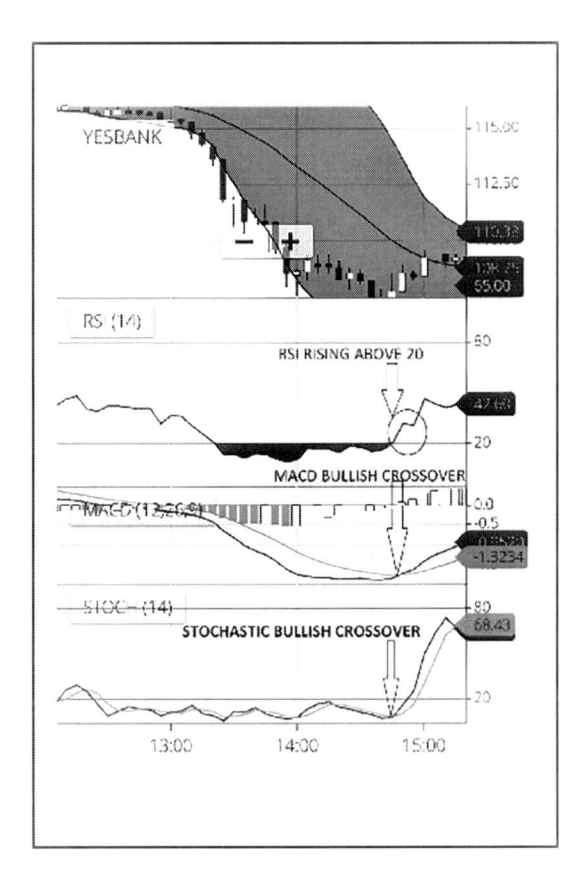

However, one must confirm that MACD crossover takes place before the stochastic crossover as the opposite may culminate into a false indication of price trend.

(vii) Trading the trends of Stochastic and MACD values

BUY when MACD is above 0 and the Stochastic indicator rises above 20 from below, falls below 20 and then rises above the recent high.

SELL when MACD is below 0 and the Stochastic indicator crosses 80 from above, rises above 80 and then falls below 80.

Limitations of the Stochastic indicator

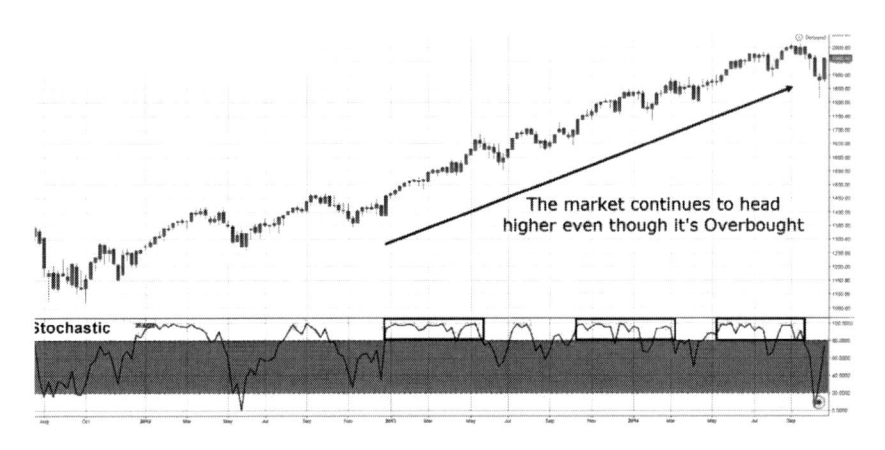

Traders must note that stochastic signals are ideal only in ranging markets and not in trending markets as the indicator's values can remain in overbought and oversold conditions for an extended period as seen in the above chart.

5. Williams %R

What is a momentum indicator?

A stock that goes up tends to continue going up and a stock that is going down tends to continue going down. The reason is that rising prices attract buyers and falling prices attract sellers with an expectation that stocks with positive momentum will tend to rise and stocks with negative momentum will tend to fall in the near future. We, therefore, need the help of a momentum indicator to assess the strength of the "momentum" of a stock's price while taking trade decisions. Among the numerous momentum indicators being used by traders to decide when to buy and when to sell, Williams %R is by far the best.

Williams %R compares the stock's closing price to the stock's high-low range over the stipulated period and tells us where the current price of the stock is vis-s-vis the highest high over the specified period and shows overbought and oversold levels. That is, Williams %R measures the capacity of bulls and bears to close price each day near the edge of the recent range.

Settings

14-days (14-periods) is the most preferred settings for Williams %R. The indicator has a range of -100 to 0.

Interpreting the readings of Williams %R

1) When the readings of Williams %R are nearing 0, it means that the current price is getting close to the highest price of the look-back period.
2) If the indicator is nearing -100, it means that the current price is getting close to the lowest price of the look-back period.

3) When the readings retract to the middle of the band, the market price is becoming equal to the average price of the selected period.
4) A reading between −20 and zero indicates that the stock is overbought or is near the high of its recent price range.
5) A reading between −80 and −100 indicates that the stock is oversold or is in the lower end of its recent range.
6) Readings between −80 and −100 are often reached. If the indicator can no longer reach these low levels before moving higher, it may be an indication that the price is likely to head higher.

Relationship between Williams %R and the Stochastic Oscillator

There is much similarity between Williams %R and Stochastic indicator, and we should, therefore, know the distinction between them.

1) Williams %R compares the security's closing price to the security's highest price over the stipulated period whereas Stochastic oscillator compares the closing price to the lowest price over the stipulated period.
2) Williams %R multiplies the above value by −100 while the Stochastic indicator multiplies the above value by 100.
3) The Stochastic Oscillator takes with it a trigger line to show the entry and exit points unlike the Williams %R.

Trading Strategies with Williams %R:

1) Trading overbought and oversold readings

As stated above, a reading between −20 and zero indicates that the stock is overbought or is near the high of its recent price range. A reading between −80 and −100 indicates that the stock is oversold or is in the lower end of its recent range. That is, readings above −20 indicate overbought zones and readings below −80 indicate oversold zones.

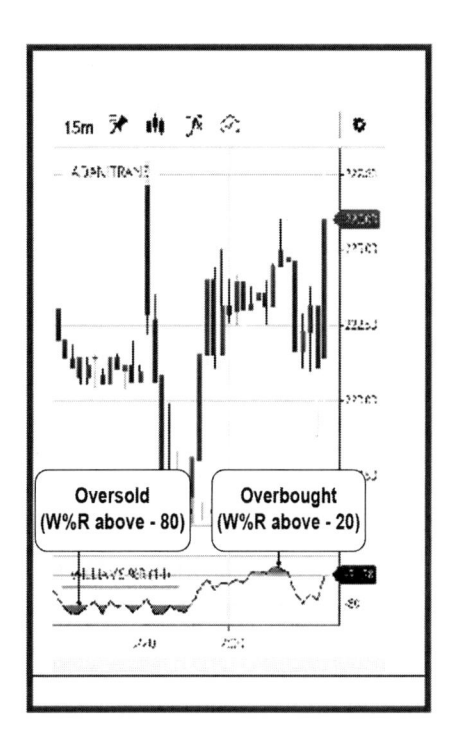

However, it is not that we should buy merely because reading is above −20 and sell merely because reading is below −80. A stock can hover around (or above) −20 when the uptrend is very strong. Likewise, a stock can wander below the reading of −80 when the downtrend is very strong. In other words, the overbought and oversold readings do not mean that a reversal is round the corner. Overbought readings actually help confirm uptrend because a strong uptrend will regularly be pushed to past higher highs and probably beyond that also. Overbought reading just means that the price is near the highs of its recent range and oversold reading simply means that price is in the lower end of its recent range. One should not, therefore, blindly take a position in the market based on the overbought and oversold readings. If your buy-sell decisions are based on price-action tools like candlesticks and the Williams %R is used to confirm the momentum in the market, it will fetch profit in all likelihood.

If the Williams %R reaches −20 and remains above it, it means that the current uptrend is strong and can be expected to last. When it gets below −20, the uptrend might be weakening and a bearish reversal is likely. Similarly, when the Williams %R is below −80, the downtrend is strong and it can be expected to last. When it gets above −80, the downtrend may be losing stream and a bullish reversal is likely.

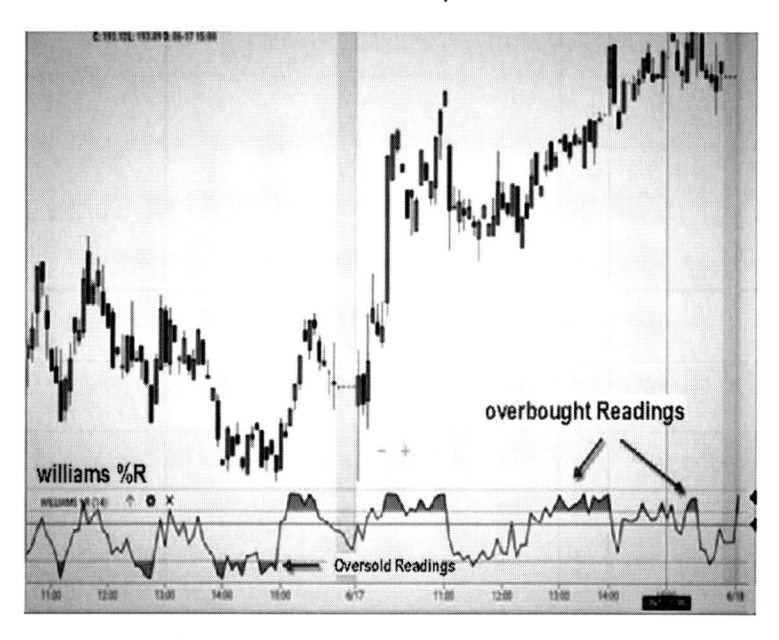

In essence, Williams %R is used to generate buy and sell signals when the readings and the price come out of overbought/oversold zone.

2) Crossing −50

The strategy is simply "Trade with the trend".

First, we should ascertain whether the current trend is an uptrend or a downtrend. How? (i) If we notice a series of higher highs followed by a series of higher lows or (ii) if a big bullish candlestick closes near the higher end of the candlestick or (iii) if the Williams %R that was in the oversold zone of below (−80) now rises to the (−50) level, in all probabilities, the current trend is uptrend and we can go long. Recent higher low may be put as stop loss. You can also keep in place trailing stop loss so that you are able to lock in the potential profits in the contingency of sudden market reversal. In the same analogy, we can go for short-selling when downtrend prevails. We must understand that

In brief, if a security, after traversing in overbought or oversold zone, now crosses the −50 line, it means that there is a shift in momentum and we can consider trading in the direction of the crossing. We must understand that momentum trading is nothing but "buying high to go higher and selling low to go lower".

3) Riding the Williams %R indicator

When a security crosses above −20 and then falls a little but remains above the reading of −30 for some time, it means that the security's primary trend is still bullish and strong and you can buy at dips and catch the primary trend early. You can ride the indicator with a trailing stop loss.

4) Trading divergence

As already seen by us in detail, when price trend and indicator's trend are in conflict with each other, divergence is said to be there.

Divergence between price and Williams %R is very powerful.

The trading strategy involving divergences has already been dealt with in a separate chapter.

5) Trading Williams %R in conjunction with Moving Averages

As already seen above, the overbought and oversold levels indicated by Williams %R are not to be blindly taken as buy sell signals. These levels actually tell us that the trend is so much strong and it is likely to get still stronger. We, therefore, take the support of moving averages in taking buy-sell decisions.

Buy when the price crosses the 100-period SMA from below and the Williams %R is above the 50 line. You are to close the trade when the Williams %R gives a closing below 50 line or the price closes below the 100-period SMA.

Short when the Williams %R is below the 50 line and the price closes below the 100-period SMA. You are to close the trade when the price closes above 100 SMA or Williams %R gives a closing above the 50 line.

6. Accumulation/Distribution Indicator

What is Accumulation/Distribution Indicator (ADL)?

If we study the quantum and behaviour of the buyers and sellers in the market instead of simply looking at price movements, we can trade more rationally and successfully. For this purpose, we should take the assistance of volume-based indicators which will tell us whether smart money is flowing in or flowing out. When we think of volume-based indicators, Accumulation and Distribution indicator takes the front seat.

The term "Accumulation" indicates the magnitude of demand for the security i.e., level of buying of the security. The term "Distribution" indicates the magnitude of supply of the security i.e., level of selling of the security. The indicator uses price data as well as volume data to find out and tell us whether a security is being accumulated or distributed.

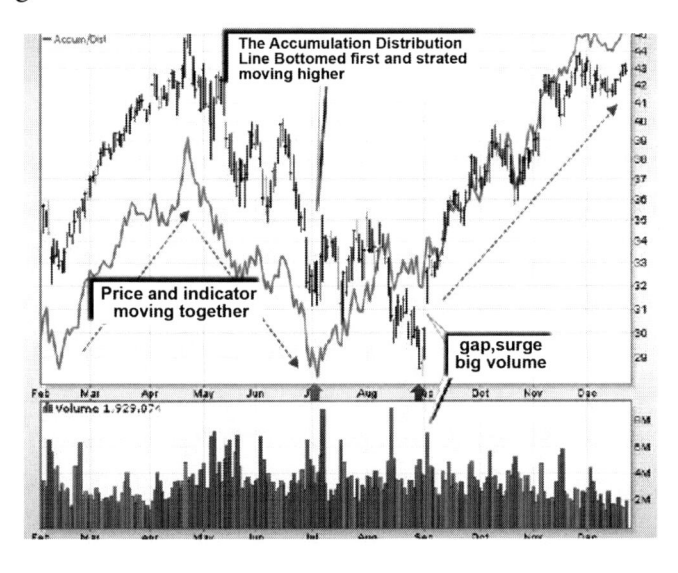

You can see in the above chart that the ADL line movement is in concert with the price movement. When the price goes low, the ADL indicator goes low, and when the price goes high, the ADL indicator goes high.

How does the Accumulation Distribution indicator work?

ADL looks at the nearness of closing prices to the highs and lows of the period i.e., the indicator sees whether the price closed above or below the middle of the period's range and thereby determines whether it is accumulation or distribution that is happening in the market. The proximity value is multiplied by volume so that price movements with higher volumes get more weight. We know that a security's volume precedes price and hence the volume traded has bearing on the rise and fall of its price. The Accumulation/Distribution indicator, being a volume indicator, predicts the direction of the volume flow and thereby predicts the stock's future price trend. The ADL will move up when the security closes near the high of its range and also with high volume. The ADL will not rise so much when the security closes near the high of the period's range but with low volume or when the security closes near the middle of the range though with high volume. Likewise, the extent of decline will be dependent upon both the volume and the extent of the nearness of close to the low of the period's range.

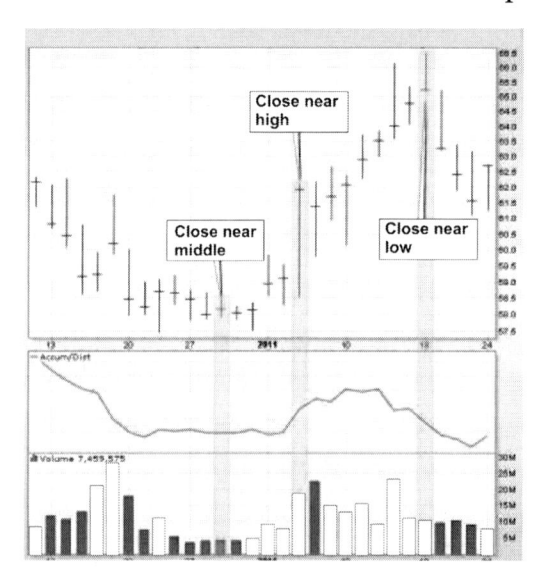

The Accumulation Distribution's actual value is not important, and only its direction is important to us.

The Accumulation/Distribution line ignores the change from one period to the subsequent period.

Calculating the Accumulation Distribution Line

The formula for calculation of the ADL is comprised of three components:

1) First calculate the Money Flow Multiplier by using the most recent period's high, low and close as shown below:

    Money Flow Multiplier = [(Close − Low) − (High − Close)] /(High − Low)

(Note that the money flow multiplier is in the range of +1 and −1. When the stock's closing price is in the upper half of the High-Low, the multiplier is positive, and if the closing price is in the lower half, the multiplier is negative. That is, the multiplier will be positive if the buying pressure is stronger than the selling pressure and vice versa.)

2) By multiplying the above Money Flow Multiplier by the volume of the period, you will get the Money Flow Volume.

    Money Flow Volume = Money Flow Multiplier × Current Period's Volume.

3) Go on adding/subtracting the new Money Flow Volume to/from the last ADL value. (For the first calculation, use Money Flow Volume as the first value).

4) The resultant figure is the ADL value.

    ADL = Previous ADL + Current Period's Money Flow Volume.

What does the Accumulation/Distribution Indicator tell you?

- If the ADL indicator for the period is rising, then the demand force i.e., accumulation may be higher, and this signals that an upward breakout is likely.
- If the ADL indicator for the period is falling, then the selling force i.e., distribution may be higher, and this signals that a downward breakout is likely.
- When both the stock price and the ADL indicator for the given period make higher peaks and higher troughs, the upward trend is likely to continue.
- When both the stock price and the ADL indicator for the given period make lower peaks and lower troughs, the downward trend is likely to continue.
- If price continues to rise while the ADL indicator falls, the uptrend in the price is likely to stall and the price is likely to start falling. This phenomenon is called negative divergence and it has been dealt with in detail later in this chapter and also in a separate chapter on divergence.

- If price continues to fall while the ADL indicator rises, the downtrend in the price is likely to stall. This phenomenon is called positive divergence.
- If the ADL line rises sharply, it confirms that the uptrend is so much.
- Strong and vice versa.

ADL vs OBV

Though both the OBV and ADL are volume-based indicators, their formulae are different. ADL sees whether the price closed near the high or near the low of the price range of the period and thereby determines whether it is buying force or selling force that is dominating the market. OBV shows whether volume is flowing into or out of a stock by finding whether the current close is above or below the prior close. It is important to note that ADL does not compare today's close with the previous close.

How to trade Accumulation Distribution Line indicator?

1) Trading the trend with ADL

You are to buy only when the ADL indicator is rising and are to sell only when the indicator is falling.

2) Divergences

Occurrence of divergence between the price and the ADL offers a good trade opportunity. For the purpose of profitable trade with divergence between the price and the ADL, let us recapitulate what we learnt about divergences in an earlier chapter:

- **What is divergence?**
  Normally, both the market price and technical indicators move in the same direction. But occasionally they don't make simultaneously higher highs or lower lows; the market price goes one way and the indicator goes another way. Price reaches a new high or new low but the **indicator** fails to follow suit and moves in the opposite direction. That is, the market and the technical indicator are "diverging" one from another. Divergences are normally indications that reversal of price trend is imminent because, as said earlier, momentum changes direction before price does and hence bullish and bearish divergences in the RSI/Stochastics/MACD/ADL indicators and price can be considered as a prelude to trend reversals.

When there is a new low in the security's price but not on the indicator such as MACD, Stochastic, ADL and RSI, it may be an indication that the downward momentum behind the falling prices is drying up and the prices will soon adjust. It is called bullish divergence. In the chart above, price is making a lower low while the ADL is making a higher low which is probably an indication that starting of an uptrend is likely.

Similarly, if the security's price goes to a new high but the indicator does not, it may be an indication that the momentum behind the rise in prices is waning, and price will soon adjust. It is called bearish divergence. In the above chart, price is rising while the ADL is falling, which may mean that accumulation (buying volume) is not adequate to sustain the price uptrend and a downtrend may start.

However, please understand that divergence is only a warning that the trend has slowed down and it does not mean that the price trend will reverse; a stock can continue to rise or fall for a long time even when a bearish/bullish divergence has occurred.

3) Confluence with other indicators

As ADL has certain limitations as seen above, it could not be the sole indicator to be depended upon for taking trade decisions.

Any trade decision based on ADL must be supported by price action tools like candlesticks or momentum oscillators like Stochastic or trend indicators like MACD histogram.

Limitations

i) Trades based on divergences when market is trending often lead to losses as trend reversal signals of technical indicators are not dependable in trending markets and ADI is not an exception. That is, ADL is working well in range-bound markets and not in strongly trending markets. To obviate this risk, traders are to follow the golden adage "Trend is our friend" meaning that we should always trade in the direction of trend only; if the market has been rising sharply, we will look to buy only, and if the market has been falling sharply, we will look to go short only. To be more perfect, we will buy when the bullish market pulls back against the trend and then resumes the uptrend. Likewise, we will go short when the falling market sees a retracement and then resumes the downtrend.

ii) The ADL indicator takes into account only the proximity of closing price to the high and low of the given period and thereby determines whether it is accumulation or distribution that is occurring in the market. As such, the ADL will rise even when the security falls gap down and closes much lower but the close is above the midpoint of the high-low range.

7. On-Balance Volume (OBV)

What is On-Balance Volume (OBV)?

Volume is the main force behind markets since volume precedes price. A period's volume is considered positive when the current close is above the prior close and is considered negative when the current close is below the prior close. Volume on up-days is added to the running OBV total and volume on down-days is subtracted from the indicator. Thus the OBV value increases or decreases each day depending upon whether today's closing price is higher or lower than the close of the previous day. That is, On-Balance Volume (OBV) line is simply a running total of the positive and negative volumes. And naturally, the indicator shows whether volume is flowing into or out of a stock. Eventually, it works well in predicting the future movement of the stock.

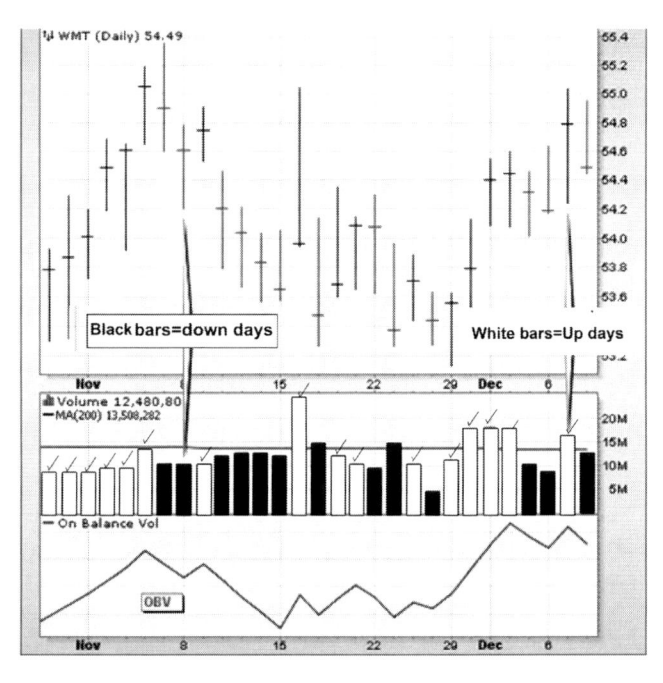

The logic behind the OBV indicator

Because of the process of adding up days' volumes to the running OBV total and subtracting the down days' volumes from the OBV total, the OBV indicator's trend should naturally correspond with the current price trend. That is, OBV should normally rise in up trends and fall in downtrends.

Calculation of OBV Indicator

OBV is calculated as shown below:

- **When today's closing price is higher than yesterday's close**

    Current OBV = OBV (yesterday) + Today's volume

- **When both the today's close and the yesterday's close are the same,**

    Current OBV = OBV (yesterday)

- **When today's close is less compared to yesterday's close**

    Current OBV = OBV (yesterday) − Today's volume

However, you need not manually calculate the values as the charting softwares in all the trading platforms do this calculation for you.

How OBV indicator works

Institutional funds like mutual funds and pension funds are the main forces that are moving the markets. These funds are much active on low-volume days while the less sophisticated retail traders are much active on high volume days as explained below:

When market is in downtrend and retail traders are in selling mode, institutional traders start buying and accumulating the stock. Volume increases but price remains relatively low. At one point, buy orders outweigh sell orders and price starts rising. Seeing the upward movement of price, retail traders start buying at the increased price with the fond hope of reaping profit at still higher prices. But now institutional traders start unloading the stocks and book profits and the not-so-sophisticated and gullible retail traders are caught napping.

To be brief, institutional funds accumulate stocks when they are inexpensive, the demand volume outweighs supply volume, price starts rising and the retail traders, seeing the uptrend, start buying and the institutional traders unload their holdings and book profits.

Interpretation

1) The numerical values of OBV are not important. The values may be positive or negative or high or low but it is only the OBV line's direction that is important to generate trade signals; the right axis of the OBV indicator need not be looked at at all.

2) We saw that OBV increases when volume on up days exceeds volume on down days and OBV falls when volume on down days exceeds volume on up days. Naturally, increasing value of OBV (indicating positive volume pressure) is likely to lead to rising prices. Similarly, decreasing OBV values (indicating negative volume pressure) is likely to lead to falling prices. Naturally, if price rises or falls in line with the indicator, the prevailing trend is confirmed.

3) If both price and OBV are making higher peaks and higher troughs, it means that buyers are stronger than sellers and the upward trend is likely to continue. When both price and OBV are making lower peaks and lower troughs, it means that sellers are stronger than buyers and the downward trend is likely to continue.
4) If there is a significant increase or decrease in volume while there is not such a change in price, the heavy buying or selling is likely to result in a very big rally or fall in the price move.
5) If the OBV is rising even though market is range-bound, it may mean that accumulation is taking place and an upward breakout is likely. If the OBV is falling despite the market being range-bound, it may mean that distribution is taking place and a downward breakout is likely.

Difference between OBV and Accumulation/ Distribution

Though both the OBV and ADL use volume to predict the quantum and direction of smart money, they differ from each other in the way of calculating them. OBV is calculated by adding the volumes of up-days and subtracting the volumes of down-days while ADL looks at the nearness of closing prices to the highs and lows i.e., the indicator sees whether the price closed above the middle or below the middle of the period's range and thereby determines whether it is accumulation or distribution that is occurring in the market.

Trading strategies with OBV

OBV is used to confirm the price trend of an asset and to look for divergences that are likely to be followed by reversal of trends as detailed below:

(i) Trend confirmation

Being a cumulative indicator, OBV provides confirmation of the direction of a trend. When the OBV indicator is steadily rising, the stock's price is likely to rise correspondingly.

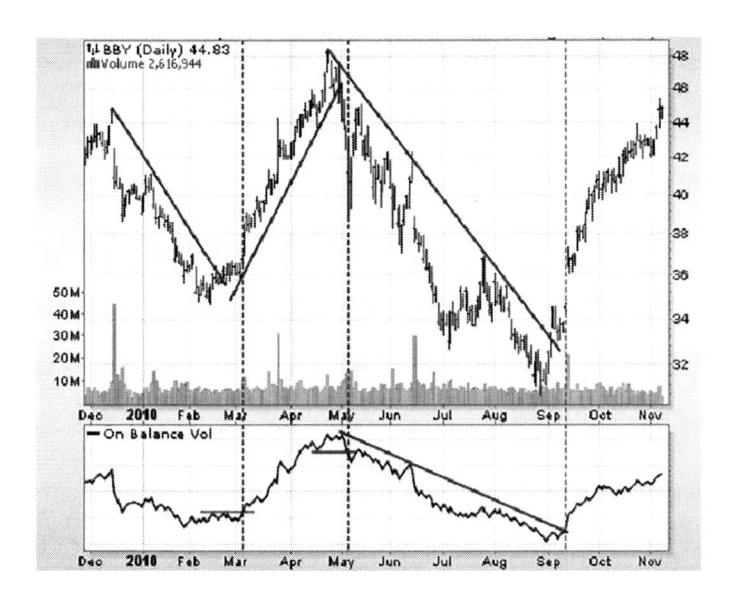

(ii) Trading divergences

If volume increases without corresponding rise in the price, an upward price move is likely to follow. Similarly, if volume decreases without corresponding fall in the price, a downward price move is likely to follow.

In other words, if price is making higher peaks while the OBV does not follow suit, the uptrend in price is likely

103

to stop and a downtrend is likely to start. This is called a negative divergence or bearish divergence. If price is making lower lows while OBV does not make lower lows, the downtrend in price is likely to stop and an uptrend is likely to start. This is called a positive divergence or bullish divergence. These divergences between price and OBV are, therefore, signals to traders that trend reversal is likely.

Limitations of OBV indicator

1) The quantum of volume being added/subtracted to arrive at the OBV remains the same irrespective of the extent of price move made during the period, and hence the change in the OBV does not reflect the magnitude of change in price.
2) OBV does not give any cue to entry points.
3) OBV with a short time frame sends many false trade signals.

8. Money Flow Index (MFI)

Price and volume data are very essential inputs to predict price movements. Money Flow Index (MFI) fulfills this requirement. It uses price and volume data to measure the inflow and outflow of money into a security over a given period of time. It does this by simply comparing the traded value of up-days to the traded value of down-days and giving the values in a percentage. Here, Traded value = Average price × Volume.

With the data of flow of money into the asset, traders can easily find out whether demand for the asset is increasing or decreasing i.e., whether there is buying pressure or selling pressure for the asset.

As MFI uses volume besides price and as volume precedes price, it does well in picking tops and bottoms in markets and thus works as a leading indicator. Naturally, it could be used to predict trend reversals as could be seen from the following chart.

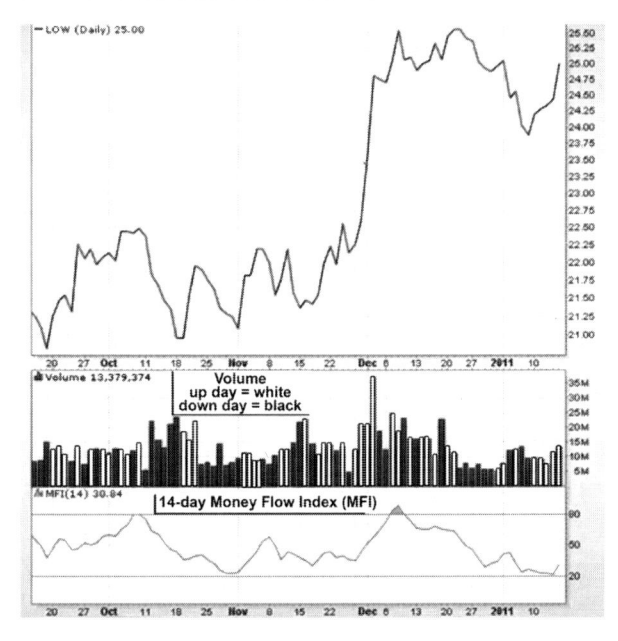

Default Settings

MFI's default setting is 14 days. MFI swings between 0 and 100 and helps identify overbought and oversold market conditions. Typically, MFI readings above 80 indicate a market top and readings below 20 indicate a market bottom.

Calculation

Although there is no need for you to calculate the indicator manually, it is better to understand the parameter settings and formula of any indicator before using it in live markets.

MFI, as a volume indicator, simply compares the traded value of up-days to the traded value of down-days and gives it in a percentage. Here, Traded Value = average price × volume.

The Money Flow Index involves a series of very simple calculations as detailed below:

- First, the period's Typical Price is calculated.

  Typical Price = (High + Low + Close)/3

- Then Typical Price is multiplied by the volume to arrive at the Raw Money Flow (also called Money Flow and not the Money Flow Index).

  Raw Money Flow = Typical Price × Volume

- If today's Typical Price is greater than yesterday's Typical Price, it is considered Positive Money Flow. If today's Typical Price is less than yesterday's Typical Price, it is considered Negative Money Flow.

  Positive Money Flow is the sum of the Positive Money over the specified number of periods. Negative Money Flow is the sum of the Negative Money over the specified number of periods. Positive money flow indicates increase in typical price implying buying pressure; negative money flow indicates decrease in typical price implying selling pressure. In other words, a positive money flow implies that traders are building up positions on the underlying security and a negative money flow implies that traders are exiting positions on the underlying security.

- Now comes the Money Flow Ratio which is calculated by dividing the Positive Money Flow by the Negative Money Flow.

  Money Flow Ratio = (Positive Money Flow)/(Negative Money Flow)

- Lastly, the Money Flow Index is calculated using the following formula.

  Money Flow Index = 100 − 100/(1 + Money Flow ratio)

Here you must note the following:

- Money Flow (i.e., Raw Money Flow) is positive when typical price rises from one period to the next period, and is negative when typical price shows declines from one period to the next period.
- If the typical price remains the same as that of the previous bar, we are to ignore that bar and proceed. That is, the Raw Money Flow values are not used when the typical price remains unchanged.

The logic behind the MFI indicator

The logic behind the MFI indicator is as follows: When the MFI increases, it means that that buying pressure for the stock is increasing, and hence price is in rising mode and traders can consider going long. And when the MFI declines, it means that buying pressure for the stock is decreasing and hence price is in falling mode and traders should consider going short. Thus you may easily predict the directional movement of the market by simply watching the MFI.

Difference between MFI and RSI

As already seen, RSI incorporates only price to find out whether an asset is overbought/oversold while MFI incorporates volume as well as price for the purpose, and thus the MFI indicator is nothing but a volume-weighted variant of RSI.

Moreover, as MFI works with price as well as volume while RSI works with price only, MFI is able to deliver trade signals earlier than the RSI as volume precedes price. In other words, MFI works as a leading indicator.

Trading MFI signals

MFI generates valuable trade signals when the following events occur:

1) Overbought and oversold signals.
2) Divergences.
3) Failure swings.
4) Trend pullbacks.

1) Overbought/Oversold condition

Being tied to volume, MFI is able to identify overbought and oversold conditions i.e., unsustainable price extremes and reversals. Generally, if the MFI of the security is above 80, the security is said to be in overbought condition and if the MFI is below 20 MFI, the security is said to be in oversold condition.

However, those oversold/overbought conditions are not adequate ground to buy/sell; the prices may continue to rise beyond 80 if the upward trend is so strong and may continue to fall below 20 if the downtrend is so strong. Traders should, therefore, seek the confirmation of the MFI's trade signals by other technical indicators.

Anyway, you ought to be alert when the MFI rises above 80 as this overdue level may be followed by retracement. If the MFI is above 80, a short trade can be considered when its MFI value falls below 80. Similarly, when the MFI falls below 20, you have to be alert and avoid/reduce short positions as it is an oversold level and price may rise. Here, a buy trade can be considered when the MFI rises above 20.

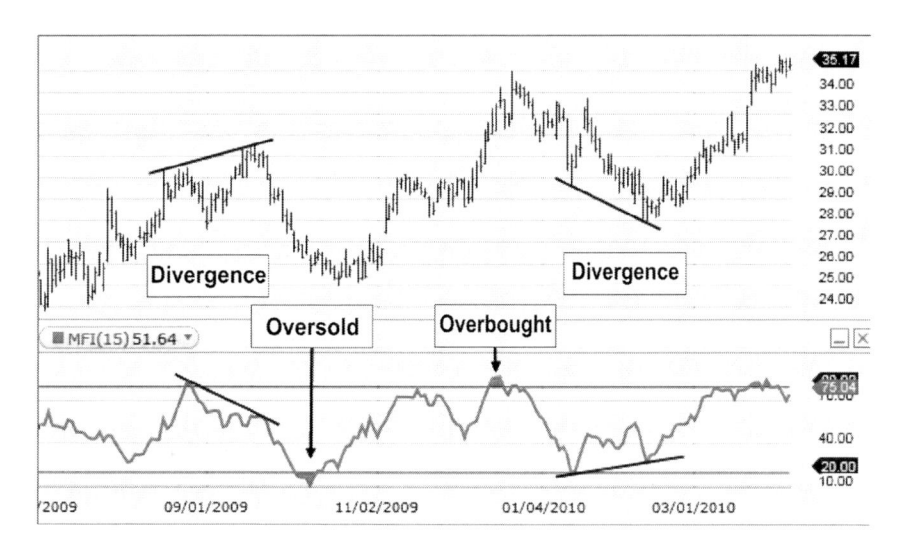

But it is to be noted that securities crossing above the level of 80 or below the level of 20 is rare.

2) Divergences

One of the main occasions of trading Money Flow Index is when there is a divergence. A divergence is said to occur when the oscillator is moving in the opposite direction of price. This is an indication of a potential reversal in the current price trend.

In other words, when the price falls to a new low while the MFI forms a higher low, it is an indication that money flow is increasing i.e. buying pressure is increasing, selling pressure is decreasing, the downtrend is weakening and uptrend gets stronger. This phenomenon is called bullish divergence, and it is a good opportunity to buy at low prices and make profit. Likewise, when the price rises to a higher high while the MFI indicator forms a lower high, there is a bearish divergence. It indicates that money flow or buying pressure is decreasing, the uptrend is weak and the current trend is not dependable; bearish divergence is a good opportunity to go short.

3) Failure swings

Like divergences, failure swings also result in reversal of price trends.

There are four steps in an incidence of a failure swing.

A bullish failure swing is said to have occurred when MFI falls below 20 and becomes oversold, recovers and rises above 20, again falls but stays above 20 on a pullback and then shoots above its previous high. This is a good buy signal.

A bearish failure swing occurs when MFI rises above 80 and becomes overbought, falls below 80, slightly increases but fails to exceed 80 and then drops below the previous low. This is a good sell signal.

4) Trend pullbacks

Suppose a security is in an uptrend and a short-period decline below the MFI value of 20 or 30 occurs and then a rally occurs. It indicates that a pullback is over and the security resumes the uptrend. It could be the time to enter a buy trade. Similarly when a security is in a downtrend and a short-duration rise pushes the MFI value up to 70 or 80 and then the security falls below the value 70/80, that could be the time to go short in anticipation of resumption of the downtrend.

5) MFI trading Strategies in conjunction with other technical indicators

(i) MFI with SMA

BUY when the price line crosses 20-period simple moving average from below and MFI crosses the 4-line from below.

SELL when the price line crosses the 20-period SMA from above and MFI crosses the 60-line from above.

(ii) MFI and MACD

If the MFI gives an overbought signal, we will go short after a bearish MACD crossover occurs. Similarly, if the MFI gives an oversold signal, we will go long after a bullish MACD crossover occurs. We will exit when the MACD crossover in the other direction occurs.

iii) MFI and momentum-based indicators like RSI and Stochastics

As seen earlier, MFI is a volume indicator, and as volume precedes price, MFI is largely a leading indicator delivering early signals. However, it must be combined with another momentum oscillator like Stochastics and RSI whose signals will act as confirmation signals to the MFI signals. If the other momentum-based indicators signal a selling while MFI is declining, the probability of the stock price falling would be much higher. Likewise, a trader can take a long position when the MFI is rising and the other indicators also generate a buy signal.

9. Commodity Channel Index

Description

The Commodity Channel Index measures the difference i.e., the distance between the current price and the historical average price of a security and thereby evolves a measurement for the strength of the trend. That helps determine whether a security is in overbought/oversold condition or whether it has taken to a new trend and whether traders can enter/exit a trade or avoid taking positions.

The momentum-based oscillator gained its name as it was originally used for commodities markets though it is now being effectively applied to stocks, indices, ETFs and other securities.

The following are the important CCI events:

- When the CCI rises above +100, it is a bullish event.
- When the CCI subsequently falls below the +100, it is an event signalling the end of the previous bullish trend.
- When the CCI falls below −100, it is a bearish event.
- When the CCI subsequently rises above the −100, it is an event signalling end of the previous bearish trend.
- When the CCI is above zero, it indicates that the price is above the historic average. When the CCI is below zero, the price is below the historic average. It can also be said that HIGH POSITIVE CCI readings indicate that prices are far above their historic average. It is an indication of strength. LOW NEGATIVE CCI readings indicate that prices are far below their historic average. It is an indication of weakness. In this manner, CCI can be used to identify overbought and oversold levels.
- CCI values of +100 to −100 indicate that market is not trendy but range-bound only, and do not send any trade

signals. Also, 70% to 80% or all price fluctuations fall within +100 and −100 as measured by the index. Buying and selling signals occur only when the +100 line (buy) and the −100 (sell) are crossed.

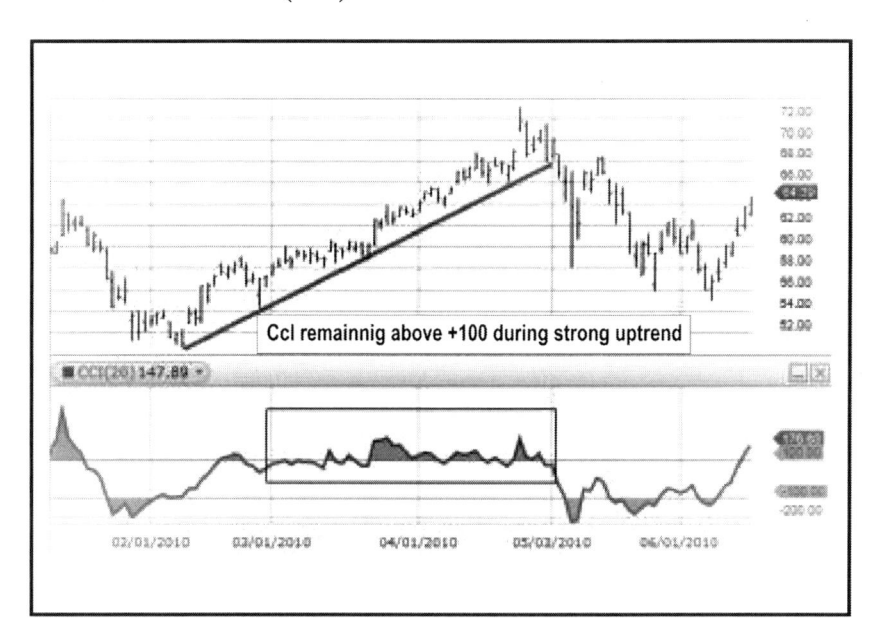

Calculating the CCI

The Commodity Channel Index (CCI) is calculated in the following steps:

i) Determine the difference between the Average Price (also called Typical Price) and the SMA of the Average Price over the period chosen.

ii) This difference is compared with the average difference over the period. (Comparing is done with the purpose of allowing for the security's volatility)

iii) The result is multiplied by a constant (to ensure that most values fall within the standard range of +100 to −100.

Formula

First, decide on the number of periods that the CCI is to analyze. Look-back period for the CCI indicator is generally 20 periods which means that the calculation takes into account price data for the preceding 20 periods. If a shorter period is applied, the sensitivity of the indicator will increase and, consequently, the number of signals will increase.

Commodity Channel Index = (Average price − SMA of the Average Price)/(0.015 × Mean Deviation) where Average Price (also known as the Typical Price) = (High + Low + Close)/3

(The 0.015 constant is to ensure that 70–80% of CCI values fall within the +100 to −100 range. The constant of 0.015 applied in the formula mostly ensures that about 70 to 80% of CCI values fall between −100 and +100. This 70 to 80% depends on the above-described look-back period also. A shorter-period CCI will have a smaller percentage of values falling between +100 and −100, and a longer-period CCI will find a higher percentage of values falling between +100 and −100).

Obtain Mean Deviation by subtracting the most recent 20-period average of the typical price from each period's typical price.

(The number of periods used for the calculations of the SMA and mean deviation are the same as that is used for CCI.)

Sum the absolute values of these numbers ignoring minus signs.

Then divide the resultant figure by 20.

This calculation is to be repeated as each new period ends.

The indicator's formula appears to be complicated, but you need not calculate them manually and memorize them; it is enough if you understand the rationale behind the indicator and learn how to interpret it, how it works and how it is used in trading.

Trading Strategies with the CCI indicator

The CCI oscillator signals to traders about important occurrences like overbought and oversold conditions, divergences, and emerging trends which are the major trading opportunities as described below:

1) Trading at overbought and oversold Levels

We already saw that when the CCI is above +100, the price is above its average and when it is below −100, the price is below the historical average. Then the simplest way of telling how to trade CCI is:

- Buy when the CCI exceeds +100.
- Exit if the security falls below +100.

However, one should not rush to trade in a jiffy when the CCI rises above +100 or falls below −100 as a strong trend may cause that the overbought/oversold condition lasts for a very long period. As CCI is an unbound oscillator with no upper or lower limits, a security can continue going higher and higher though the CCI shows it in overbought condition. Similarly, the security can continue moving lower and lower even after the CCI shows it in oversold condition. That is, overbought and oversold levels are not fixed but subjective and a security is considered overbought or oversold when its price reaches a relatively extreme level though −100 +100 may work in a range-bound market. In other words, more extreme levels of reading are required for a security to be considered overbought or oversold. That extreme depends on the historical range for CCI and the volatile nature of the security. Volatile securities entail higher extremes than static securities. Therefore, traders look to past readings on the indicator to get a sense of where the price of the security is often reversed. They note the prices at which trend reversals have often taken place and the CCI readings at the time of those reversals. One particular stock might have witnessed most of the reversals near +200 and −175. But another stock might have had most of the reversals near the CCI readings +350 and −320.

However, in a majority of the cases, −200 and +200 are considered sufficiently harder levels to represent true extremes well.

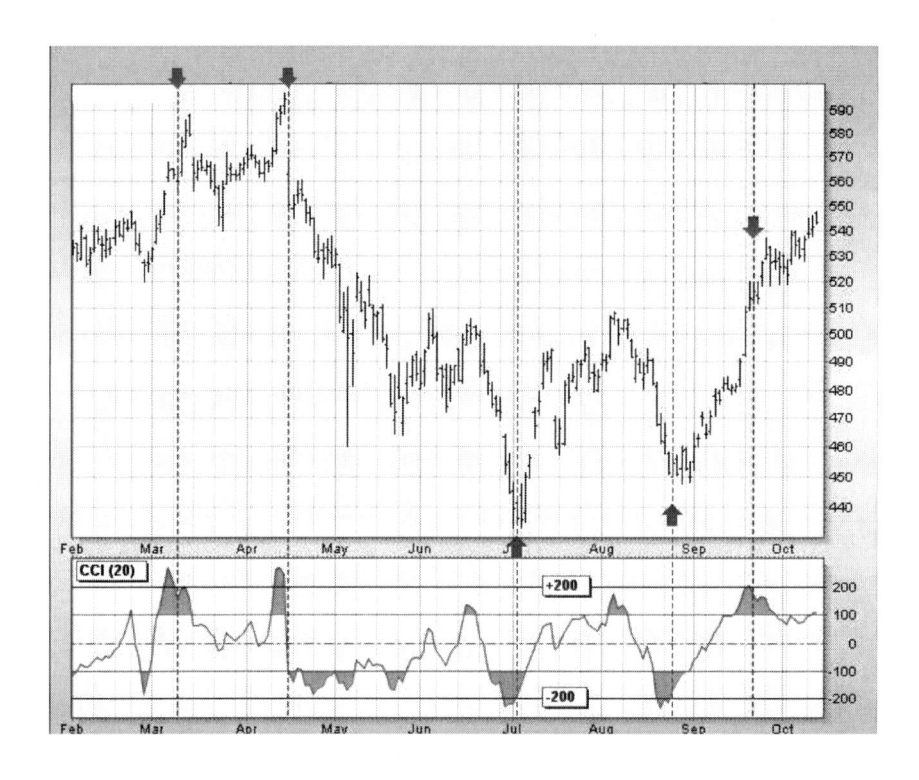

2) Trading when a security goes out-of-bounds and gets back

When the CCI oscillator goes out of bounds and gets back, traders consider it an opportunity to trade. For instance, when the CCI crosses +100 from below but falls back below it, traders consider going short. Similarly, when the CCI falls below −100 but rises above it, traders consider going long. The above chart also shows these price movements.

3) Trading potential extended move

We had seen earlier that during 70% to 80% of the time, the CCI will move within the range of −100 and +100. During the remaining 20% to 30% of the time, CCI will be outside the range of −100 and +100 which is an indication of unusual strength/weakness in the current market trend. This condition of CCI moving outside the range of −100 and +100 is a signal of a prospective extended move offering trade opportunity.

4) Identifying Emerging trends

When the CCI rises from negative (or near-zero) territory to above +100, it may be an indication of the beginning of a strong new uptrend, a rally in both CCI and price signalling a buying opportunity. Similarly when the CCI moves from positive (or near-zero) readings to below −100, it may be an indication of the beginning of a strong new downtrend signalling to quit long positions or to go short.

5) Divergence

We already saw about divergence in detail in a separate chapter.

Occurrence of divergence between the price and the CCI indicator offers a good trade opportunity. For the purpose of profitable trade with divergence between the price and the indicator, let us recapitulate the things we learnt about divergences in an earlier chapter:

- What is divergence?
  Normally, both the market price and technical indicators move in the same direction. But occasionally they don't make simultaneously higher highs or lower lows; the market price goes one way and the indicator goes another way. Price reaches a new high or new low but the indicator fails to follow suit and moves in the opposite direction. That is, the market and the technical indicator are "diverging" one from another. If the security's price goes to a new high but the indicator MACD/Stochastic/RSI/CCI does not, it may be an indication that the momentum behind the rise in prices is waning, and price will soon adjust. Similarly, when there is a new low in the security's price but not on the indicator, it may be an indication that the momentum behind the falling prices is drying up and the prices will soon adjust.
- Divergences are normally indications that a price trend reversal is imminent because, as said earlier, momentum changes direction before price does and hence bullish and bearish divergences in the RSI/Stochastics/MACD/CCI

indicator and price can be considered as a prelude to trend reversals.
- However divergence is only a warning that the trend has slowed down, and it does not mean that the price trend will reverse; a stock can continue to rise/fall for a long time even when a bearish/bullish divergence has occurred.

6) Trend line breaks

When a trend line drawn connecting the peaks and troughs breaks out and simultaneously CCI crosses above −100 from oversold level, it could be considered a good opportunity to go long. When CCI at overbought level declines below +100 and there is a trend line break, it could be considered a good opportunity to go short.

7) Confluence with other technical indicators

As CCI is an unbound oscillator with no upper or lower limits, securities can continue going higher though the CCI readings show it in overbought condition. Similarly, the security can continue going lower even after the CCI readings show it in oversold condition. Hence trade the CCI in combination with additional indicators to identify overbought/oversold conditions. CCI is a momentum oscillator and hence one more momentum oscillator would be redundant. A volume indicator like the Accumulation Distribution Line and the On-Balance Volume or a trend indicator like moving average and MACD will make a good pair to the CCI in arriving at right the trading decisions.

Let us see below how to trade CCI in conjunction with moving average, MACD and Parabolic SAR.

(i) CCI and MA

Trading CCI in conjunction with a moving average improves the signals' quality. Here, the moving average line will act as a support and resistance line.

Buy when the CCI comes out of the oversold territory and climbs above the −100 mark and the price line crosses the moving average line from below.

Sell when reverse conditions are met.

(ii) CCI and MACD

Buy when CCI leaves the oversold territory and rises above −100 and MACD crosses the signal line from below.

Sell when reverse conditions are met.

10. Chande Momentum Oscillator

What is the Chande Momentum Oscillator?

The oscillator calculates the difference between the sum of all recent gains (i.e., recent higher closes) and the sum of all recent losses (i.e., recent lower closes) and then divides the result by the sum of all price movements over the same period. In other words, it measures momentum on both up days and down days. The result is multiplied by 100 so that the indicator oscillates between +100 and −100. The timeframe applied for the oscillator is usually 20 periods.

Calculating the Chande Momentum Oscillator indicator

1) Calculate the sum of higher closes over the given periods.
2) Calculate the sum of lower closes over the given periods.
3) Subtract the sum of lower closes over the given period from the sum of higher closes over the same periods.
4) Add the sum of lower closes over the given periods to the sum of higher closes over the same periods.
5) If the current close equals the previous close, it is to be ignored.
6) Divide the result of the above (4) by the result of (3) and multiply by 100.

$$\text{Chande Momentum Oscillator} = \frac{SH - SL}{SH + SL} \times 100$$

Where

SH is the sum of higher closes during the given periods and SL is the sum of lower closes during the given periods.

7) Plot the above value.

However, you need not do these calculations as the trading/charting softwares will take care of the calculation part.

Interpreting the Chande Momentum Oscillator

1) CMO measures the strength of trend. Higher absolute values of the CMO indicate that market is trending and the trend is stronger. Lower absolute values indicate that trading is range-bound/sideways. Traders are, therefore, able to take their cue from these values in predicting the strength or weakness of the future trend. The following chart shows lower absolute values of CMO going hand in hand with range-bound market.

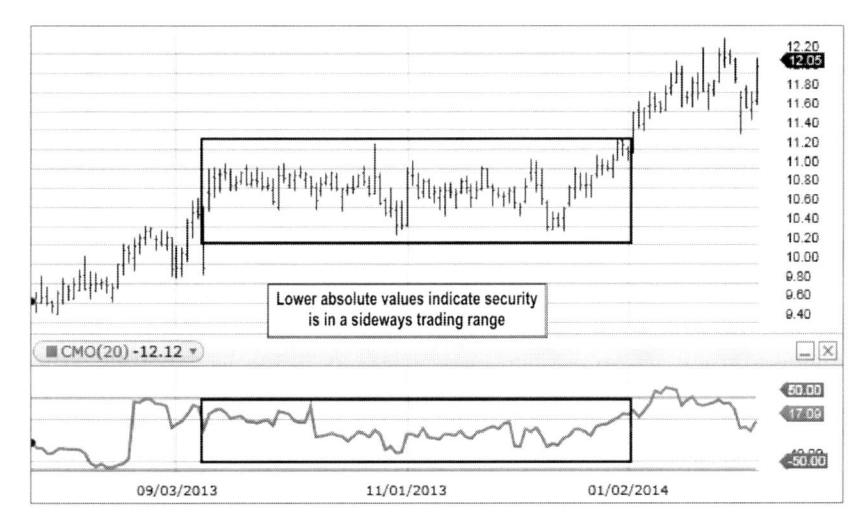

2) If the CMO is oscillating between the zero line and +50, it means that market is in a strong uptrend. If the CMO is oscillating between the zero line and −50, it means that the market is in downtrend.

3) An asset is considered overbought when the CMO is above +50 and oversold when it is below −50.

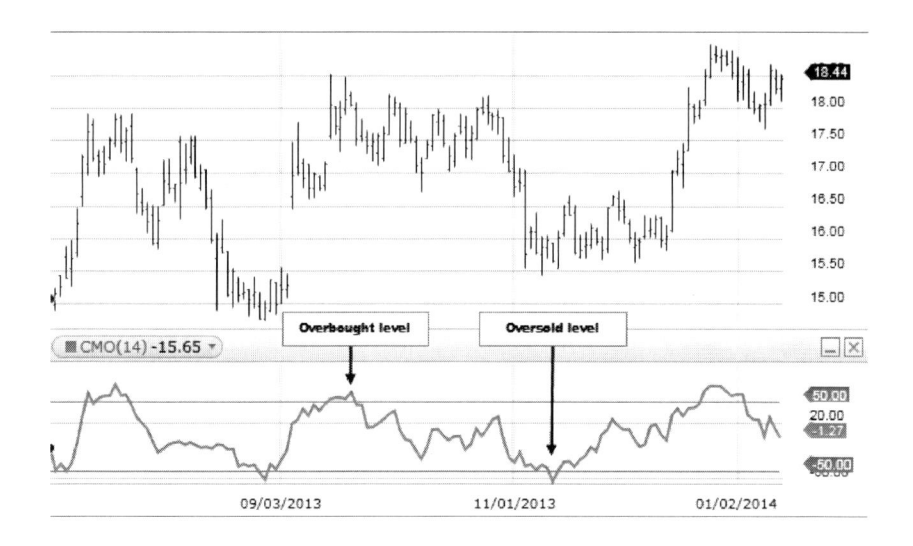

Trading with Chande Momentum Oscillator

1) The simplest way of stating the trading strategy is "Sell when the CMO rises above the overbought level of 50 and buy when CMO falls below the oversold level of −50".
2) Some traders bring to the charts page a 10-period moving average of the Chande Momentum Oscillator to signal entry points. When the CMO crosses that moving average line from below, a buy signal is generated, and when the CMO crosses the moving average line from above, a sell signal is generated.
3) A buy signal is generated when a short-timeframe moving average crosses a longer-timeframe moving average from below. The buy signal can be acted upon when the CMO gives a confirmation signal by crossing the 0 line from below. Similarly, the CMO's crossing the 0 line from above can be taken as a confirmation signal to sell when a short-timeframe moving average crosses a longer-timeframe moving average from above.

Divergence

Occurrence of divergence between the price and the CMO offers a good trade opportunity. For the purpose of profitable trade with divergence between the price and the CMO, let us recapitulate what we learnt about divergences in an earlier chapter.

What is divergence?

Normally, both the market and technical indicators move in the same direction. But occasionally they don't make simultaneously higher highs or lower lows; the market price goes one way and the indicator goes another way. Price reaches a new high or new low but the indicator fails to follow suit and moves in the opposite direction. That is, the market and the technical indicator are "diverging" one from another. Divergences are normally indications that reversal of price trend is imminent because, as said earlier, momentum changes direction before price does and hence bullish and bearish divergences in the RSI/ Stochastics/ MACD/ ADL/ CMO indicators and price can be considered as preludes to trend reversals.

When price is making a lower low while the CMO is making a higher low, it is probably an indication that starting of an uptrend is likely. It is called bullish divergence.

Similarly, when price is rising while the CMO is falling, it may mean that buying volume is not adequate to sustain the price uptrend and a downtrend may start.

However please understand that divergence is only a warning that the trend has slowed down and it does not necessarily mean that price trend will reverse; a stock can continue to rise or fall for a long time even when a bearish/ bullish divergence has occurred.

Limitations

As the oscillator does not smooth results, it triggers oversold and overbought conditions very frequently, and hence buy-sell decisions are to be taken only after confirmation by price action.

Conclusion

In the process of improving your skill in trading techniques, you should not be too obsessed with technical indicators and should not be adding to the chart more and more indicators as such adding of too many indicators will entail processing of too much data and information which will lead to analysis paralysis and will complicate your trading activity. You must, therefore, resist the temptation of having too many cooks.

Manufactured by Amazon.ca
Acheson, AB